Climb the Highest Mountain

by

Gene Edwards

SeedSowers Publishing
P.O. Box 3317
Jacksonville, FL 32206
www.seedsowers.com

SeedSowers Publishing
P.O. Box 3317
Jacksonville, FL 32206
www.seedsowers.com

Dedication

To the young men who first heard these messages and lived them into reality.

You were about twenty in number; your average age was 22. I have never known, nor will I ever know, an honor greater than this: I served with you in Christ.

It is my hope that I will one day see some of you again. I trust, in that future hour, I will see you as I saw you in your twenties . . . high up on a mountain . . . with a banner in your hand . . . and a gleam in your eye.

Contents

The Story Behind the Book

This is a book on a subject that no one wants to write about, division in the body of Christ.

I was converted to Christ at age seventeen, and yet I had already witnessed two major church splits (and several minor ones) *before* I was a Christian!

For a while now I have been taking an informal poll of Christian workers. Based on my highly unscientific findings I would venture to say that a Christian worker can expect to pass through a minimum of three major – catastrophic – splits by the time he reaches fifty. So will the typical Christian.

A church split will constitute one of the major events of *anyone's* life. Your chances of spiritually surviving, intact, just *one* split in your lifetime is probably less than 50 percent.

I do not believe in division in the body of Christ for any reason (The *possible* exception would be sexual immorality that was being countenanced.) The *true* reason for division and the stated reason for division are never the same. The heart of man is too deceitful for any of us to trust anyone causing division.

But though I do not believe in division, alas, it happens anyway! I would venture that of the 300,000* protestant congregations in the United States, a minimum of five to ten thousand will divide in the next twelve months, affecting the lives of at least a million professing believers.

We really should not ignore a problem this enormous, and this tragic. (Perhaps, if this book accomplishes nothing else, it will cause wise men somewhere to begin taking this skeleton out of the

*As of 2000 A.D.

closet and dealing with it for what it is, a major problem in the Christian family.)

In the late 1960's, I stepped out of a more formal setting of the Christian faith into that infinitely smaller area of informal Christianity. In this tiny little world of Christians I found some of the dearest believers, some of the most precious groups and, certainly, the purest and most noble of all Christian workers. But I have also run across, it seems, more nuts, kooks, and screwballs than in all my years of working with thousands of pastors and Christian workers in dozens of countries who are within formal Christianity.

I hasten to add that Christians outside the structured church experience division far more than those within, and far more than would ever be expected for their small numbers.

This book is about many things, but mostly it is about division. I hope it will help Christians in the mainstream of the protestant faith, and the little nameless groups who meet in homes. But it is for the latter I carry the greater concern. Small, unstructured groups do not have safeguards the are naturally found in organized denominations. The carnage of division "outside formal Christianity" is absolutely appalling. I trust this book will play some small role in eliminating some of this division, and in comforting those who have already drunk of the bitter cup.

The circumstances under which the messages which constitute this book were delivered, have been kept a closely guarded and undiscussed secret for many, many years. It is still a little unnerving to sit here and disclose a small part of the story, but you have the right to know the surrounding drama, else the message of this book will be lacking. And it was very much a drama! This book, then, is a series of "on-site" messages delivered just prior to a division.

In order to be clear, I must gather up some seemingly unrelated events and weave them together so that you may see how those events all converged.

I was converted to Christ during my junior year in college. At that very time a revival was sweeping America. It is sometimes referred to as the post-war revival. One thing stands out clear in my memory: That revival, like most revivals, lasted four years (not counting the foregleam and afterglow); nonetheless, it seemed that virtually every fervent-hearted, visionary Christian I met in the next ten years had been converted in that brief period.

Exactly 20 years later, when I was 37, another revival swept across America. That revival also lasted about four years. The messages you are about to read were delivered during that revival.

The revival I saw at age 17 was quite unlike the one I observed at age 37. The first one was flashy and youth-oriented. Big choirs, spotlights, flashily dressed speakers. It took place about the time when America was "inventing the teenager!"

Perhaps the major outcome of that revival was the beginning of the acceptance of the interdenominational Christian organizations. The Navigators, Campus Crusade for Christ, Youth for Christ, Young Life – *all* came into prominence and acceptance at that time.

Like all American revivals, it was typified be fervor, by multitudes being led to Christ and by a few prominent names and movements emerging. Sad to say, little attention was paid to developing spiritual depth, and as a result little was gained. This was to have great impact on the next revival.

For the record, I personally recall that season – shallow or not – as precious and treasured days.

The second post-war revival, the one in which these messages were delivered, was unlike any other revival in America's history. This revival, like virtually all revivals, began spontaneously among young people; but it was the *only* revival this country has ever seen which took place outside the confines of structured Christianity.

The revival began among young people; it was leaderless and directionless. It was personified by those beautiful, unbelievably messy things called "Jesus Houses." In towns and cities all over America, big, barny houses were rented out by newly converted Christian young people all living together. Typically, all helped with meals and expenses; there was a lot of care, love, acceptance, an atmosphere of community and of tolerance, marked by a wonderfully simplistic Gospel. There was also a non-sectarian atmosphere of Christian acceptance, the like of which has been hard to find in the annals of church history. To put it another way,

the doctrinal and denominating barriers that have so long charac-
terized Christianity had not yet been raised among those dear young
people.

It was pure, refreshing and beautiful. But it wouldn't last.

And what caused its demise? For one thing, the results of
the first revival met the results of the second. Here's what I mean.

There was a leadership vacuum in this new revival and a
directionlessness that was bound to spawn a new element in its
development. This new element was the entrance of older men –
ambitious, for the greater part unbroken – men with backgrounds,
with doctrines, with denominations, with the need to protect, to
lead, to adjust.

On the other side were thousands of young Christians caught
up in the enthusiasm of experiencing the Lord's blessing and ready
to believe whatever they were told. The stage was set for this new-
ness and openness to give way to the forms and practices of older
men.

The eventual fate of this revival was evident. The time of
innocence passed. The refreshing spontaneity and informality of
the Jesus people gave way to defined ways of doing things. Walls,
barriers, fears, "groupism," "elitism," "sectism" – all were insemi-
nated into that revival through the ancient, shallow, threadbare convictions, doctrines, forms, rituals and practices of older men and
bygone days.

Movements large and small would come from this revival.
The openness that had existed between little fellowships around
the country was gradually replaced by the fear that a visitor might
be a "wolf." As men "protected their flocks" tests of fellowship
mushroomed until they became legion.

And after all that?

Well, unfortunately, older workers seem not to understand
that their young followers do not stay young, nor naive, nor gullible
forever. Eventually a few men and women *in every one* of those
groups – upon reaching age 30 – would begin to think for themselves, see themselves as having been duped, misled, used and
abused! Rightly or wrongly, righteously or wickedly, out of flesh or
out of spiritual (or maybe only psychological) wellsprings... these

iv

followers would turn on their leaders.

The eventual power play, the predictable division, the vicious words and splintering of most of these groups signaled the end of what had started out as a uniquely different and blessed work of God.

Was such an end inevitable? Will it always be? Or could some of those young Christians have been spared the disillusionment and heartache that awaited them?

I personally feel – and I ask no one to join me in this conviction – that the greater need, *then* and *now*, is for the emergence of a new kind of worker. Workers who, in times of revival, will give young believers Christ instead of doctrines, who will build walls out of Christians rather than between them. Then could the ravages of division be abated. To present a whole new standard for the Christian worker *and* the believers, is the purpose of this book.

That brings me to the group of young people to whom these messages were first delivered. Please be assured, dear reader, that they were no more, and possibly a whole lot less, "spiritual" than their counterparts around the nation.

The place was a tiny, obscure village, population 4,000. (Well, 4,000 in the summer; but come September and the opening of school, it mushroomed to a gigantic 16,000.) There began in this little town, a small group of Christians. They were the remains of an international campus Christian organization that had ceased to operate on that campus. Virtually unnoticed and unknown, they grew to about 20 in number. Their seeking after the Lord had led them to desire an experience of what was then called "body life." They were a close-knit leaderless "non group" of young people. To say they were free, unstructured, open and spiritually ignorant is to give new meaning to the term, "Brother, that's putting it mildly."

One day I would meet this erstwhile little group. And the likelihood of our becoming fast friends would seem remote, indeed. Our backgrounds, at least at first glance, would have less in common than oil and water. They were studied and dedicated gentiles; mostly out of the "hippie" generation. I, in turn, was of the tribe of Baptist – not only a Baptist of Baptists, but I received my citizenship by birthright (Southern Baptist, three generations, both sides of my family). A year after my conversion, I entered a Southern Baptist seminary, pastored for 5 years and then became a Southern Baptist evangelist.

Surely, if the story stopped there, Those Christians in Isla Vista and I would have been oil meeting water. But something happened to me at age 30. As a minister, I found myself in a crisis of conscience. There were three elements in that crisis.

First, my view of the body of Christ was widening. Eventually I felt I could not continue to denominate myself within the community of believers. I wanted to, I needed to, lay down all barriers to other Christians.

Secondly, I was going through a quiet agony over this thing we call "church." Travelling a lot, I think, had been the thing that provoked this problem in my life. As an evangelist I had met so many Christian workers and spoken in so many churches of so many denominations. I was absolutely overwhelmed by the enormous gap that lay between the expression of the church in our age as over against the expression of the church in the first century. This was not a crisis of doctrine nor belief; this was a crisis of practice. Little by little, I found my heart dreaming of other ways the church might express herself.

The third element in this crisis had to do with an ache in my own heart to know Christ better. I had come to a crisis that had to do with my own spiritual depth, or lack thereof. This sense of spiritual need became a relentless cry inside me, a quiet agony, With all my love and respect – then and now – for my rich Baptist heritage, I speak historically when I say that we Baptists have never been known for our great spiritual depth. There was no place within my own heritage to go to assuage this inner thirst.

Incidentally, the second element and the third element in this crisis kept bumping into one another. That is, I wanted to see and experience a higher expression of church life. I also wanted a far deeper walk with Jesus Christ. Putting these two together, I hoped to find a deeper experience of Christ *within* a higher experience of the expression of the church. Finally, I dreamed of seeing *both* these elements among a gathering of believers who knew and practiced no barriers. No sectarianism. No "talk one way, practice another."

As I said, it was a crisis of conscience. For the heart to long after any one of these as reality is a crisis. All three at once constitute a *very* large crisis. Eventually, this crisis would culminate in my laying down all ministry in which I was engaged.

The crisis was compounded further by background. I had then, as I do now, a sincere and profound respect for my Baptist heritage, upbringing and training. (Until this day I have difficulty perceiving myself as anything except a Baptist minister who works for a living, who instead of meeting in a "church building," meets informally with Christians who gather in homes).

Eventually, though, I made a decision. It was the simplest possible decision: I would lay down all ministry in which I was engaged. To put it another way, it was a decision to see the proverbial cart go out of service until such time as the horse could be up front where it belonged. I would know Christ in a far deeper way than I had known Him, before I would ever minister again. Ministry without a deeper knowledge of Christ was of no importance to me. To know Him was all-important. I would know Him better; whether or not I ministered again was His business.

Shortly after I made that simple decision, something quite remarkable happened to me. Now, a statement like that generally makes people sit up expectantly.

A vision?

An empowering?

Prophetic utterings?

Nope.

The Lord chose a far more effective method of transformation. Pain. Pain that would profoundly affect the rest of my life. I contracted a very deadly, very destructive disease. I spent the next year in bed; not at all sure I'd see my next birthday, much less the restoration of church life.

The next three years following found me only slightly better.

Four years of almost total waste.

Do *not* underestimate the ways of *God*.

Eventually I regained a semblance of health. But the point was not wasted on me that my desire to know Him better had led me to four years of bed rest and a body forever shorn of strength.

It was just at this time, when the Lord was allowing a bit of health and strength to flow back into my body, that I received an invitation to come visit that unusual little group of college Christians in that unusual little village of Isla Vista.

I did not learn this fact until much later, but their invitation to me was sort of a last hope. They had exhausted all other resources and really didn't know where to go from there for practical help nor light on "the body" and how it worked.

We were both a mess. It was love at first sight!

Please mark this: Here was that naive, leaderless, directionless group of free Christians; and in walked "the older Christian worker." History paused to repeat itself; but, dear reader, that beat-up, feeble Baptist minister and that little group of Christian young people *did not* – did not – repeat history.

I accepted the invitation to visit the Christians in Isla Vista. From time to time I came back. Then at the end of a few months I sat down and had a serious talk with them. Essentially, this is what I said.

"I will come to visit you from time to time for one year. I will do all I can to point you to Christ...to know Him, to experience Him and to know His cross. I will endeavor to continue to show you the church and how to experience church life as a living reality in your daily lives.

But at the end of one year I will leave. And having departed, I will stay away for at least one full year."

Now why would I choose to help a group of young Christians in the matters of Christ, and the body of Christ, for one year and then leave for one year? The answer has something to do with missiology, specifically with that fascinating way in which Paul of Tarsus raised up churches against insuperable odds and in the face of impossible circumstances.

I refer to Paul's almost unvarying approach to *church*

planting:

He would enter a city where Jesus Christ had never even been named... and he would spend (an average of) six months to one year in that city. While there, he laid a foundation of *Christ* in the lives of a motley group of former pagans. At the end of this brief period of time he left them. (He was usually chased out of town.) He often did not get back to that city – and to that church – for one or two years.

And note this, please read the record very carefully, he departed from those churches leaving them without elders or leaders. At the time he left them, they were still an unstructured, unled people. (Elders usually got appointed in these churches on Paul's *second* visit.)

And during this crucial period of the church when Paul was not present and leaders did not exist, the church always seemed to be assaulted with unbelievable problems and crises. And it turned out, in *every* case the church would survive.

Paul made a comment about this fact. It went something like this:

> "Every man who raises up the Lord's house can be sure that a day of testing will come. His work will be tried by fire. If he lays a foundation of, and builds with, wood, hay and stubble, then in that day of fire his work will burn.
> " I built with silver, gold and precious stone; fire cannot destroy these."

Paul built with Christ, and later in the hour of fire, the churches were not consumed.

I had seen a lot of wood, hay and stubble burn during my life as a Christian worker. I had also seen an awfully lot of men trying to do everything in their power – in the inevitable hour of division and fire – to keep their work from burning. Invariably, their efforts to prevent division and crisis seemed only to add to the magnitude of the problem.

I had set myself, then, this goal: For one year, I would seek to build among those young Christians with material which was incombustible. I would seek to build with nothing but Christ. I wanted to know, at the end of that year, if that group of young Christians could survive and remain in good shape a year all alone and utterly unprotected.

This was no small order, as we shall see.

Back during that period in my life between the time I laid down the ministry and when I began working with those young people in Isla Vista, I had spent a great deal of time looking at the ministry of Paul of Tarsus. I was overwhelmed with how Christ-centered was his ministry. Not just in word, but experientially. That man, as his people, was centered in Christ. How incredibly deep was their experience, how awesome their strength. And all this depth and strength of foundation was imparted, experienced and made real in such a very, very short time.

And later, against the worst assaults of darkness, each church managed to survive.

Quite frankly, it seemed to me, such a Christ-centered ministry, such an imparting of spiritual reality ought to be the goal and standard of every Christian worker. I was determined it would be mine.

Paul had some pretty scrubby converts – gentile pagans – for his "laboratory" where he could test his theory of *Christ as all*. In a very real way, so did I. The hypothesis had the right place and the right people and the right circumstances for a genuine testing ground!

Here were 20 young people, all about 21, all very recent converts, with virtually no Christian background. Many, if not most, had come out of the drug culture or the revolutionary movements of that time. Yes, true, certified *gentiles!* What they knew about the depths of Christ could have easily been written on the side edge of a small piece of paper. Furthermore, they lived in a one-square-mile community that was perhaps one of the most drug-oriented square miles in America. It was also probably one of the most immoral (or was it amoral) too. The university located there was the philosophy arm of the state's university system. Over the years the school and the community had taken on a very aggressive anti-Christian attitude.

Needless to say, to live corporately for Christ in such an

environment was bound to cause a stir!

It wasn't uncommon for our meetings to be interrupted or invaded. We had windows smashed, car tires slashed, bikes stolen and... oh... you probably wouldn't believe it if we told you the rest.

Anyway, I spent about 100 of the next 365 days with those young believers. During that time we met together a great deal, sat around and talked a lot, sang more than can be imagined, and prayed a considerable amount.

The first year together was rich and wonderful. It was a glorious and memorable experience. The Lord did a great deal to win our hearts.

The spoken ministry touched none of the peripheral doctrines of the Christian faith. I fear, in my rush, I left out a few central ones too. I sought to major on Christ, on experiencing Him, and on His cross.

One night, we fell to discussing the revival that was sweeping America. I shared with them some of the things I felt would be the result of this revival. I concluded with a comment to this effect: "Let's sit out this revival. It is a great opportunity to grow large and spread, etc. But I believe we should sit out not only this revival but also the whole next decade! Let everyone else have this decade. Let's just hide. And grow up together. Then, maybe we will have the wisdom and experience to well care for the 1990's! Surely, by then, you will have something of Christ to impart."

Well, at last, that first golden year drew to a close and it came time for me to depart.

I was fearful (scared is a better word) and hopeful. I deliberately left them with few (if any) guidelines for survival. They had not the foggiest idea of elders and leaders. I figured that Paul of Tarsus, leaving town just a few steps ahead of a mob, had given precious little advice to his converts – and appointed *no* leaders. I would deliberately do the same.

By the end of the year we had grown to about 70 in number. All were terribly young and totally gullible. Anyone with a toothy smile and 5 good sermons could have easily sold them Mecca, Rome, New Delhi or the Brooklyn Bridge.

I had promised to leave, stay gone, not return and in no

way interfere for one full year. Could they last? Would they be there, one year later when I returned? Is so, in what kind of shape would they be?

Well, as are almost always the ways of God, the totally unexpected happened. To say the least, I got my wish. That obscure little group of Christians in Isla Vista had about as much fire to rain down as could possibly be imagined. (The only thing was, it just didn't happen *when* I thought it would.)

I will tell you a very small part of the story. It is a story neither known nor told until now. Even those young Christians caught up in the vortex of it, have never told it, nor heard it. As I have already stated to you, the event is recorded here because, otherwise the book, *Climb the Highest Mountain*, would be far less than it ought to be as a book.

Let us go aside now to another city and another people. The place is the headquarters of one of the largest Christian organizations in the United States, A division – a terrible split – is taking place. There are stated issues, but as human psychology and splits go, it was actually more a power struggle between two men. The charges of the one leading the split were that the organization was too legalistic, too structured, too authoritarian.

Soon they launched a movement of their own, made up of leaders and students who had left that organization. The new movement was, of course, unstructured. It developed a message that was an extreme view of grace. Their doctrines and concepts were to pass through many stages. And as they did, each stage became more and more radical. Their idea of the church at one point, could probably have been summed up in the following comment: "If God wants people to meet, He will tell them so and He will tell them where to meet and what time the meeting starts."

Ultimately the movement and its message began to disintegrate. Their message of grace was producing, in the extreme, swearing, cursing, drunkenness and immorality. The movement skyrocketed into chaos and collapsed leaving hundreds of Christians – leaders and followers – disillusioned, confused, bitter, with the ability to vent their hostility, generally toward leadership.

Now, what does this have to do with 70 young Christians

in Isla Vista?

Just before I made my departure from these young college believers, one of the Christians from that strange "grace" movement came and began meeting with them. Just *one* person, but he happened to have been a major factor in the now defunct grace movement. During the next 12 months many of his friends and followers moved there, too, the number of them eventually reaching nearly 100.

(I was leaving just as things were about to get interesting!)

Things went smoothly for the first part of that year I was away. But as more and more of these Christians arrived, there was a definite shift in attitude. Some of them were highly gifted and nationally known leaders. Many were strong willed. All were hurt. Some were incredibly bitter. And in all was still that divisive nature, that bent toward controversy, that boast in past dare-doings... and, still, under the surface – a predilection to violence, moral license, and in some, an incredibly vulgar language.

Nor, it later turned out, had they lost the gift of sowing discord and creating division in the body of Christ. In the beginning, some had arrived there for the purpose of being healed. Some came out of curiosity. Others came to defy. Most of those people, having moved in while I was gone, had never met me nor even *heard* of me. Nor I, them. I was a name only. To *them* that name stood for some sort of leadership, be it ever so benign. Gradually, I began getting a message, just a trickle, then loud and clear: "We don't know who you are, but whoever you are, you are not welcome to come back here."

There were now, very definitely, 2 separate groups who just happened to be meeting under the same roof. One group was about 20 to 23 in age. The other anywhere from 24 to 40. One group was incredibly naive, The other, older, was gradually becoming once again a restless, cohesive group. Older, wiser, but as much prone to divisiveness as ever.

It was to *this* situation I would return.

Some scene huh?

My limitations are without number, but I am not stone dead. And anyone my age would have to be *that* dead not to see what was going to happen. The original little band of innocent kids was about to plunged into a fiery ordeal of the first magnitude.

At that time I had 2 or 3 deeply held feelings about division in the body of Christ and what my role should be in the midst of such a division should one occur.

Belief number one: Division is inevitable, It is a test of our hearts. Number two: When division threatens a work, the worker should not interfere. He should let it happen... because, after all, it *will* happen. He may delay it, and he may even mistakenly think he has stopped it, *but division will come!* Belief number three: A worker should build so that fire cannot burn the work. *And* if it does burn up, there in the inevitable holocaust, *he surely ought* to be the first to know, to want to know, *and* to *admit*, that *he has built with wood, hay and stubble.*

I held, and hold, a worker ought to wish to know the answer to this question: *Have I built with combustibles or non-combustibles?* There is no way to know, except in crises. To always protect a work, to ever be launching a crusade against dissenters, is to never know of what composition is your building material.

Christ, or hay – of which have we built? Fire alone can tell. I believed – and still believe – that when a work (that is, a church) which is experiencing church life is about to be plunged into a crisis the worker should leave! (It is not only the most honorable thing to do – the only faith-filled thing to do – but it is the one thing the worker can do to minimize damage. Just try *staying around* and see what happens!)

Come back when the fiery trial is over! Scrounge around in the ashes and see if you can find, there in the rubble, a *little* precious metal that did *not* burn.

Granted, that is *not* your commonly held view of what a Christian worker should do during a crisis in the kingdom of God. But I felt then, and now, that the highest, the best and just possibly the most scriptural course a worker can pursue is to leave town.

If the Christians who are left in the chaos of a division have learned the cross and if they have seen Christ, *a division is not a dangerous perilous* thing to go through. True, a split can be a brutal, hurtful, damaging thing when there are two sides. But only if there *are* two sides. I had, or at least I hoped I had, shown a group of young people how to take the cross in all things. If my premonition about an impending split was correct, I would soon find out just how well they took Christ in the face of dissension and chaos. Would they go to the cross… and there die?

These were the thoughts that were uppermost in my mind as I contemplated a return to a fellowship of Christian believers, half of whom I had never met and did not want me to return.

Well, the day arrived for my wife and me to return to Isla Vista. We returned by air. I have no shame in telling you I sat there in my seat and cried the entire flight. I had a boundless dread of what awaited us once we stepped off the airplane.

The next weekend a meeting – a retreat for the men – was held in the mountains that lay above Isla Vista. The place was a Presbyterian conference ground named Rancho La Sherpa. There were 40 men present. About half of them were new to me. The other half were those young men I had grown to love the year before.

So, dear reader, you now know the background of the messages you are about to read. They were delivered high up on a mountain, to a group of young men who were probably about to be plunged into an inferno. It was a call to them to rise up to a new standard of conduct in the face of devastating division. I had some hope the schism might not occur, that these messages might turn the tide away from a split, *but* realistically it was more probable that this *might* turn out to be my last opportunity to address those young hearts… for I was committed to *walk away* if and when a split began to build. These messages were possibly my farewell address!

"And did the sundering occur?" It did. A little later.

"And did you leave when it started?"

I left – again – just before the split began. "And was it bad?"

The word *savage* might be more descriptive.

"And the young men? And the young women? Their conduct? Did they meet the standard? Did the banner move?"

The banner moved.

I am certain of few things. But of this I am certain: That banner moved. They faced that horrible hour with no earthly aid nor counsel and with no past experience by which to plot their course. And they survived by the grace of God. They made into reality the messages that you are about to read.

And they survived!

Perhaps I should share this small story that you might get a glimpse of how a group of Christian young men and women handled an extremely volatile situation... spontaneously and instinctively. And *alone!* I was speaking to one of the dear sisters in the Lord who went through that decimating hour. Here, in essence, is what she said about that experience as she recalled it to mind.

> "You know, we were all kids, we didn't know *anything* about situations like that; yet not once in all that time did anyone refer to what was happening, I never mentioned it to anyone, not even my roommates; nor did they ever say anything to me. None of the brothers, either – even the ones taking the brunt of it. As far as I know, not one person among us ever said even one word to one another about what was happening. And in all the years since then, I've never heard anyone refer to it, and I don't think anyone else ever has. As far as I know it has never been mentioned."

It was a violent catastrophe, yet in a few months the whole thing was behind us. Within a year, it was virtually forgotten.

There *are* better ways than those now abroad in the land by which Christians can handle church crises.

About four years after these messages were delivered; they were put out in pamphlet form. I recall one letter from a reader who said, in essence, "You are presenting an ideal which is too ethereal; it will not work in reality." Well, it had already been lived out in reality by a group of about 70 young Christians, It was they, not I, who proved a that it is *not* necessary to go through a schism with all that interplay of vicious words that produce so much hurt.

There is an alternative:

You can lose!

You can let things be destroyed.

You can die.

May the Lord hasten the day when more Christians choose such a walk in the presence of division.

And now, I trust, with this introduction, you will find these messages a bit more meaningful. I hope you will accept them into your own life in a very personal way. I trust that in the course of reading them you will make some private decision in your own heart about your walk in that future hour of extreme crisis *you will* face someday in the body of Christ. Be sure, the crisis is out there. Be sure you will face it. Be sure, your heart will be tested, and your heart *will* be revealed.

And by your conduct in that hour,, angels will know (in Paul's words) of what you were constructed.

> Now if any man build upon the foundation (Jesus Christ) with gold, silver, precious stones, wood, hay straw, each man's work will become evident; for the day will show it, because it is revealed with fire; and the fire itself will test the quality of each man's work

1Cor. 3:12-13

The Lord *will* send that hour into your life, The hidden motives of your heart *will* be tested. What will be your walk?

*   *   *   *   *   *   *

I waited fourteen years before writing this book. Were I to deliver again today the messages which you are about to read, their content would be somewhat altered. I would weigh several statements more carefully. I would leave out a few things. I might even add a little, I would rephrase much. Many statements about structured Christianity, I would very definitely temper. You find the messages here as I gave them then, not as I would today, since I am perhaps a bit mellowed by age.

One last word. Some books give their main point in the beginning and then slowly fizzle. Other books build, the latter part of the book being the most valuable. Part III of *this* book is definitely the most important portion.

And now, dear reader, should you and I one day chance to meet, I would trust in that hour you, too, will have a banner in your hand and a gleam in your eye… for there are many more mountains that need to be scaled.

Gene Edwards

time did anyone ever refer to what was happening. I never mentioned it to anyone, not even my roommates; nor did they ever say anything to me. None of the brothers, either — even the ones taking the brunt of it. As far as I know, not one person among us ever said even one word to one another about what was happening. And in all the years since then, I've never heard anyone refer to it, and I don't think anyone else ever has. As far as I know it has *never* been mentioned."

It was a violent catastrophe, yet in a few months the whole thing was behind us. Within a year it was virtually forgotten.

There *are* better ways than those now abroad in the land by which Christians can handle church crises.

About four years after these messages were delivered, they were put out in pamphlet form. I recall one letter from a reader who said, in essence, "You are presenting an ideal which is too ethereal; it will not work in reality." Well, it had already been lived out in reality by a group of about 70 young Christians. It was they, not I, who proved that it is *not* necessary to go through a schism with all that interplay of vicious words that produce so much hurt and damage.

There *is* an alternative:

You can lose!

You can let things be destroyed.

You can die.

May the Lord hasten the day when more Christians choose such a walk in the presence of division.

And now, I trust, with this introduction, you will find these messages a bit more meaningful. I hope you will accept them into your own life in a very personal way. I trust that in the course of reading them you will make some private decision in your own heart about your own walk in that future hour of extreme crisis *you will* face someday in the body of Christ. Be sure, the crisis is out there. Be sure, you will face it. Be sure, your heart will be tested, and your heart *will* out.

And by your conduct in that hour, angels will know (in Paul's words) of what you were constructed.

> Now if any man build upon the foundation (Jesus Christ)
> with gold, silver, precious stones, wood, hay, straw, each
> man's work will become evident; for the day will show it,
> because it is *revealed with fire*; and the fire itself will
> test the quality of each man's work.

I Cor. 3:12-13

The Lord *will* send that hour into your life. The hidden motives of your heart *will* be tested. What will be your walk?

*   *   *   *

Fourteen years is a long time. Were I to deliver again today the messages which you are about to read, their content would be somewhat altered. I would weigh several statements more carefully. I would leave out a few things. I might even add a little. I would re-phrase much. Many statements about structured Christianity, I would very definitely temper. You find the messages here as I gave them then, not as I would today, since I am perhaps a bit mellowed by age.

One last word. Some books give their main point in the beginning and then slowly fizzle. Other books build, the latter part of the book being the most valuable. Part III of *this* book is very definitely the most important portion.

And now, dear reader, should you and I chance one day to meet, I trust that in that hour you, too, will have a banner in your hand and a gleam in your eye ... for there are many more mountains that need be scaled.

Gene Edwards

Part One

Part One

CHAPTER 1

Three Groups in Church History.
To Which Do We Belong?

Flip through a Church history book, and you are struck by one thing: from 325 A.D. to about 1500 A.D. all you read about is Roman Catholicism. Beginning about 1500 A.D. there is a second stream, Protestantism. But is that all there is to Church history? Is there no more? Are we so bad off that the entire history of the Christian faith has nothing to speak of but Roman Catholicism and Protestantism? (I don't need to tell you that Protestantism today does not look much like the church did during the first century.)

There *is* a third line, a third group of people. Go back and pick up that Church history book again, and this time read the *footnotes. There* it is you will find the third line. It is made up of Christians who stood outside organized religion.

Who are they? What is their story?

Look at them carefully because they foretell . . . *our* mission! (When you learn about *them,* you begin to see *our* place in history, our reason for existing. That is the reason I wish to begin these messages on our mission by looking first at history.)

Theirs is the most beautiful saga in Church history — the hidden Christians of the ages! Their story is the rich, compelling story of men who lived a primitive faith. The saga is unparalleled in the annals of mankind.

Don't look for one group, or an unbroken line. Don't look for the mythical "Apostolic succession." You will not find it. They have existed in every century since 325 A.D., but in every century their story is a little different. The first group appeared on the scene in about 350 A.D. in Spain, of all places. Hated, despised, persecuted, this particular group survived for about 100 years. The next group arose on the island of Iona off the coast of Scotland during the 500's. There were others after them. One group was in the Baltics; in another age, there were those in the Swiss and Italian Alps; in yet another age, southern France. These little groups have been there in *every* age of Church history. They have been called by dozens of different names. They stand as a witness to the simplicity of faith in Jesus Christ.

And what was God doing with each of these peoples? Simply this: He was keeping His testimony alive. A testimony of the centrality of Christ in the universe — *His* preeminence. This is why God raised them up. This was *their* mission. And so, as we sense the purpose God had among these different peoples, we also begin to sense our place. Our mission.

Men had a work in every age, but God Himself also worked. His very own work existed somewhere on this earth in every age. His work was usually small, His people usually nameless. His work with each group, you might say, was short-lived. For one short, glorious moment they lived, and He had a work on the earth. It was like a wondrous burst of light. God would use that group for forty to eighty years, perhaps a hundred. During *that* time *He* had His people . . . and as the light faded in that group, God moved on to work again, somewhere else.

In the early ages of Church history, from 325 to 1517, you read a story of a few people keeping a dim light shining in dark ages. After 1517 the pace quickens, the course alters. Now this third force in Church history was called on to be not only a light, but also a *restoring* people: rediscovering, restoring, re-experiencing the ways of God. Restoring the experience of the first century; that is, rediscovering the full experience of knowing Christ and restoring the experience of the church.

There was restoration before the 1500's, but most records of that restoration were destroyed; so the things restored then have been lost to us. Persecution, sword and book burning saw to that. Those things, therefore, had to be restored *again* and given back to the Lord's people as a *permanent* testimony. That task has fallen to all the little groups God has worked in since 1517. In fact, *restoration* was their mission. And the truths of things restored since 1517, generally, are still available to us.

This third stream of Church history has always been small. In some centuries they numbered only a handful. But mark this: their contribution has always been overwhelming. Their light has always been great. Often, if not always, they had more light than the other two lines combined. Some of the purest truth and some of the clearest and deepest insight into Christ are found among these people. So it has been, from 325 right up to this hour. And now we come to this present hour. As a people, in which of these groups do we fit? We could stand with the Roman Catholics, or we could go join the Protestants.

Actually, we don't belong with either. We belong in the line of those outside. We belong in the footnotes. We belong among those who have stood for the centrality and the supremacy of Christ . . . in their lives, in their gatherings. These messages, then, will give you an idea of our own outlook as we step out of nowhere into that pageant of Church history. We take our place abreast of those who were determined to know nothing but Christ; to march with those little bands who were seeking a full experience of the body of Christ . . . the experience of the church!

Turn around and look back! Yes, by all means look back. Be a student of Church history. Look at those little groups who came before us. Drink deep of their experience. Learn what they went through. Read their messages. Read their history. Find out what they learned. We need to know all *they* learned. We will never get anywhere unless we know ahead of time what they have *already* discovered! We are not to begin at zero. We must begin, rather, where they left off. We *must* be students of Church history. We *must* know what God has *already* done. Find out what God has already restored! Find the issues God has already uncovered. We need to be familiar with God's past work. Why? Because we need to have some idea of what has *not* yet been done. What has been done. What has not been done. What glory gained. What mistakes made. We must know these things.

Today we step into this unnumbered throng and take our place. As we do we look back, and unashamedly we draw from the wisdom, the experience, *the mistakes* of those who have come before us.

Knowing Our Heritage

Imagine with me a great mountain. The summit of that mountain is important. That summit has already been reached. Once. Since that time others have assaulted that summit. And in every age the summit comes closer within our grasp. And now! Now you are one of those who have been called on to assault its heights. As you stand in the foothills and look up, you must realize that you don't *really* start here. Others before you have made it possible to go directly to some high outpost . . . a place where other men in the recent past came. There they pioneered. Now they have laid down their climbing gear; the camp is still. The angels wait for another group of men to take up the task. You can go directly to that campsite. It shan't take long, *if* you know the way! *If* you know what has been done before. Others have pioneered a way up that mountain for you. Much of this mountain, thank God, has already been retaken. No, the summit has not been reached again; but men have gone a long way up its slopes, further perhaps than you could realize. And at a bloody price. Be sure that any people who try to start all over again are *never* going to get anywhere!

6

You must go on to the experience of those who have already assaulted these heights and start from there.

Be clear: we must *know* what God has already done. We must know a great deal about those little groups who have come before. We must master our heritage. Now as you begin to move up the steep slopes you notice a series of banners along the way. These banners were thrust in the earth long ago by those groups who came before you. Look up the side of the mountain. Can you see a banner waving high up there — far, far above all the rest? Someone has already reached a far point. 'Tis the last outpost! In fact that point was reached not so long ago. In this century! Look into the soil. You can still see the footprints of those who came before you. Along the way you may come to think you have reached a place where no man could have reached before. Be careful. You will come to places that seem impossible to forge. But look! See, incredibly, there in the distance another banner waving high and proud! After a while, you will begin to deeply appreciate what God has already done; the enormity of the suffering, the sacrifice; the experience that has already been poured out by men seeking the heights. Eventually a sense of humility will overtake you. You will even sit down sometimes and question, question seriously, if any group of people (especially those of us who have grown up in this modern society) can ever match the devotion of those saints who came before us. Can any people in this modern age press the banner higher? As you see the places they have scaled, you wonder if we have the mettle to go beyond where they left off. In fact, I must confess, that question has yet to be fully answered! Let us hope the verdict is, "Yes!" If that is the answer, then *this* age is going to need a new breed of men. The folks who came before us gave up so much; they loved Him so much, with such an abandonment; the thought that we might catch their devotion is breathtaking!

Press on up the hill. See! The distance between the banners becomes shorter and shorter, the slopes steeper and steeper.

Even though there is not much distance between the banners yet there was as much grace (and devotion) needed to forge those short distances as there was for the long ones.

At last you come to a banner waving so high. It is in a place so remote, a place so spectacularly difficult to reach, you can hardly believe any man ever came this far! You know, instinctively you know, *"this* is where *our mission* begins." (Frankly, I can't even say how many years it will take just to get to the outpost, but I believe you will each have at least 20 to 30 years of life left in you when you reach that last campsite, that last banner.) Now turn around and look *back.* And now turn around again and look *up.* Where is the summit? Is it near or is it far away?

Unfortunately, we do not know. Or perhaps I should say, *fortunately* we do not know. God will not tell us. In His wisdom He has veiled the summit. It may be only a short dash or it may be a long way off. Maybe a few short years! Maybe generations! Maybe a few short hours. Maybe centuries. You will never be told beforehand.

And now that brings you face to face with a question. Do you dare assault the mountain? Do you dare press beyond *this* point? Is there any chance you might reach the top, the crest? Be careful. If you decide to press forward you may be buying for yourself nothing but bitter disappointment. Look back again. See all those who have come before. Remember their suffering. And *they fell* short of the summit. There are no guarantees in this business. Did they mind? Would they do it again, knowing they would not make the summit? The future is not only uncertain, but *unknown.* No man can penetrate the mist above. There are no prophets on this ridge. You may guess, but you *cannot* know.

Be certain of this - the men who came before you *suffered.* If you seize that tattered, bloodstained banner *you will suffer!*

Yes, these dear pioneers have always been praised for being the greatest Christians of their century . . . but remember that praise came several hundred years *after* they were dead and

8

buried. When they lived, *they were hated.* They were despised. They were called terrible things. That happens to hurt. Deeply. Those dear saints bore unbelievable abuse. Until that hate has piled upon you, individually, personally, you can't really imagine how awful it is. Oh, your grandchildren may stand one day at your grave and say, "If we had lived then we would have honored, not persecuted, these holy people." But that is pretty scarce encouragement when you have been dead for a hundred years. Remember that!

The Tragedies of Success; The Certainty of Failure

But there is more than just suffering. In fact, that *is* the romantic side. There was success, and with that fact I'd like to change the subject a little.

Search the records. Call the roll. Look at the names. Priscillians. Brethren. The Waldensians. The Moravians. The Little Flock. All these — and others — were at one time the center of God's work on the earth. They *were* His work. They were the vanguards of restoration. They were the standard of their age. They are those whom *God alone* raised up. But read the story as they seized the banner. They moved up the slope. One day they, too, came to a place that they *knew* was new territory. (That's an exciting moment!) Unscaled, uncharted, they knew beyond doubt that they were going where no people since the Apostles had been. They were about to accomplish what no one had ever accomplished for over a millennium. Furthermore, they sensed that the full blessing of God was on them.

Now comes the sad part. The darker side of this wonderful saga. Let's look at it. When this "new territory" is reached by a group of people, without exception, someone among them cries out, "We are it! Look at us, we are it! We *are* God's work upon the earth today! We have seen, we have experienced, what no one else in our age has seen. We know a fuller restoring of God's mystery than any other people who have come before us."

That moment is followed by another cry. A fatal moment it is. "*We* are going to be those who complete the restoration. *We* are *it*." (They do not mean that they are the only Christians on the earth. They do not mean they are the only saved ones. They mean, "We are the ones God is doing His own heart's work, His own dream, through. We are His main project on the earth today." And often: "We shall be the ones to reach the summit.") Well, saints, when you hear this, you know this isn't a proper attitude, and you know that you must not make this mistake. But don't be too critical of them, either. And don't kid yourself. We are a small group of people but we have all had these exact same feelings right here among us. Furthermore, we are keenly aware it is almost impossible to keep from having these feelings. In other words, we know what we are up against. The temptation is overwhelming. And today we are setting that very fact down in black and white! The chances are that we, too, are going to fall into this same pit. In fact it is virtually assured that we will.

So we have three huge questions before us as we stand at the foothills. First, in the light of such great suffering, do we dare press the battle for the summit? Second, do you realize the great unlikelihood of reaching the summit? Third, do you realize the great pitfalls we might fall into . . . for all those in the past *have* made terrible blunders!

For instance, we have already experienced how difficult it is *not* to feel special in the eyes of God. The truth is this: when you do break out into some new heights, and *know* you're in new territory, it is very hard not to feel special.

There have been times in our experience when young brothers among us have cried out, "We are God's work in this age."

But right now is not that moment. This is a calmer moment. And I am not a young brother who is speaking today. (Yet I do publicly confess that there is an excellent chance we are going to fall into this same trap. The temptation is well nigh irresistible.) As far as I know, everyone who has traveled this way before — for at least a millennium — has fallen into this pit. Frankly, we don't know a cure for this disease. But there is one thing we can do! Today! Here! At this retreat! We can look this awful temptation straight in the face. We *have* recognized the danger. We have stated it, out loud. We have brought this ugly villain out into the light and made him stand here. We have calculated the danger. We have warned ourselves.

Our Choices

Now the decision. Do we take the banner in hand? And if so, what is *our* mission? For God gave each of these people a mission. Well, we have already covered one point. What? We might begin by determining to stay out of that snare we just mentioned. By the mercy of God we are going to try, too; yet knowing full well our chances are somewhere between nil and zero. So maybe we shouldn't go?

That brings us to the next point. Look at our choices. They are *two*. First, stay home. Second, go . . . and fall in the trap. If we go on we are almost certain to fall into some kind of pit! So maybe it's not worth the effort! We will stay home! (Let's *not* venture out if we are going to spend our whole lifetime in fear that we will fall into some trap.)

There just may be a third possibility. We can look the danger straight in the eye, consecrate ourselves in a spirit of humility, in a spirit of teachability, and a spirit of receptiveness . . . and we can ask the Lord to keep us. We can be comforted in knowing He will drop us, anyway, when He is through with us. (And we can do all in our power to see we don't survive for too long a time after He is finished with us.)

Yes, we *can* venture out, but it is dangerous. If we do, then from this day forward, we must seek to be without spiritual pride, pretension, sectarianism or boastfulness. We do not know who we are. We do not know God's final desire. Nor our destiny.

So, should we venture out, will we plant this banner on yonder summit? Who knows! The fact is we may not get past the very first banner! But this is also a fact: it is our heart to take that banner and place it on the *highest* summit. We don't know if we will, and we will not boast. Nonetheless we have a hope: if we fail the summit, we ask a grace-filled Lord to at least give us the privilege of taking that last banner beyond its present point. *That is reward enough!*

Every once in awhile someone says, "Why, you folks are going to end up just like all the other groups. You're going to end up as a denomination; another sect. Everyone else in church history has failed before you. *And you will fail, too.* Why do you want to go and add one more tragedy to the mess? The present chaos is bad enough." We agree. Everything in that statement is true. But please, my friend, behold our choices: Stay home or dare!

If we stay home then we will simply hope that in some ethereal way we can fellowship with the whole body of Christ. We can be a glob. We will sit in the ectoplasm; a gooey, non-world, for the rest of our lives.

Or we can *dare!* Dare the dangers, chance the failure. The way is fraught with destruction. We run the risk of failing where everybody else has failed before us, where everybody else has missed the mark. Dear brother, when faced with those two alternatives, and having no other choices before us, our way is clear: WE WILL DARE!!!

Under no circumstances are we going to sit home. An ethereal, universal glob we will *not* be! We, today, will dare. We're going to look back at our heritage; we're going to look up to what is not! We are going to take the wisdom, the experience, the conquest, the victories, and the *defeats,* of those who have gone before us. We're going to use those dear saints as our map, our compass. We will not sit alone in our living room and wave at one another across the street. We will dare do what men have paid with their lives to do in ancient ages. *We will gather.* We will meet. We will *be!* And we shall be a people! With a view as wide as the horizon, and as high as the summit. And we shall have a prayer for mercy. Saints, *we have no choice.*

Take a sober, yes, *even a grim* look at the problems we face. Having done that, we must now order our lives so as to avoid the many dangers that are before us. But such a noble gesture is a guarantee of absolutely *nothing.* We have no guarantees. I would like to repeat that. *We will probably fail.* If we fail, we fail. But this one thing we will never do: we will not sit home. *We will be.* We dare.

Beside you is the banner. Before you, on a journey that could take a minimum of 50 years, is the summit.

CHAPTER 2

The Witness of the Past

Before we proceed, I would like to look again at these three streams of Church history. The first one reaches from about 325 A.D. to our present time. The names of the people involved are well known. They are Augustine, Thomas Aquinas, Loyola and the Popes. And there are even the sweet saints who enlightened that dark thing: Terese, St. John of the Cross, Guyon, Lawrence. This is Catholicism.

Then there is the second stream — Protestantism. The names there are even better known to us — Luther, Calvin, Zwingli, Knox, Edwards, Wesley, Carey, and in more recent years Moody, Mott, Taylor, Finney, Graham, etc.

But what of the third stream? Who ever heard of Waldo, Zinzendorf, Darby?

You have heard of Catholics, Lutherans, Presbyterians, Methodists, Baptists. But who ever heard of Bogomils, Waldensians, United Brethren? These are not their real names! These are names given to the nameless. You'll not find much written about them. Until the 1500's most of what they wrote was destroyed. No, there is little in print from them or about them.

Let's be realistic. Every one of these groups had their own peculiarities (some *very* peculiar indeed! . . . even outrageous). But God was not offended by their outrageous beliefs. I always think of the Quakers when I think of that fact. The Quakers did not believe in the Trinity. In fact, it was the Holy Spirit that they did not believe in as a person; nonetheless that same Holy Spirit poured out His blessing on that people for a generation. God was not offended! As you look at each one of these groups, you will notice a few factors fairly common to them all. (Present day authors frequently go back to these primitive groups and try to find their "pet" doctrine being taught "by *all* these groups." Those who are all for Bible study find all these groups studying the Bible; those who are pushing tongues find all these people speaking in tongues.

First, they each had simplicity — that's perhaps the main word. Second, *no* strong or intricate theology. Third, deeply spiritual. Fourth, pious. Fifth, hidden. Sixth, because of persecution, they met (mostly) in homes. Seventh, they refused to take a name. Eighth, they exhibited an incredible love for one another. They showed incredible mobility (they could move out of town at the drop of a sword). Most had no clergy. Most of them, but not all, also had these three traits: an emphasis on the Scripture; and because of persecution, many of them lived in common; they left no buildings and no institutions.

Another interesting thing is that the blessing of God was usually on them for no more than a generation, rarely more than three generations. But even here you find exceptions. For instance, the Waldensians seemed to have the blessing of God for *hundreds* of years, which is fascinating.

Lastly, of course, they have been more or less overlooked by Church historians. That is amazing because — from the view of heaven — they must be the very center of history.

Two other things come to my mind about this third force in Church history. And here may be the heart of the whole matter. You get this more as a *sense,* but it comes through in every letter they write and in every page you read: they seem to have an incredible, subjective sense that they *must* exist. They had an innate feeling: "We belong, it is imperative that we *are.*" They gladly were tortured and killed because they would not give up the matter of their simply feeling they needed to exist on the earth. Often, with no doctrine to defend or cause to stand for, they died at stakes because they simply knew they had to be. Some kind of sense they had of a need of a testimony in dark days. It's intangible, but it was there. The other thing you note, perhaps the most obvious thing, is they almost universally (but not quite) *experienced genocide.* The history of the ''nameless'' believers is a story of torture and a story of death. Many of these groups were totally removed off the face of the earth. Often one group gave up hundreds of thousands to the most cruel means of death. It is a bloody, bloody story.

And will this be the lot of all such groups? I do not know. There are exceptions. The Plymouth Brethren have gone largely unpersecuted. They have suffered little loss by death. On the other hand the Waldensians, the Albigensians, the United Brethren (Hussites) were almost totally annihilated. The Swiss Brethren, the Bogomils and the Priscillians were even more so.

(Frankly, I don't expect us to suffer the way the Swiss Brethren did. Or even the Little Flock. I doubt that we will, generally, pay with our lives. But I *do* expect the possibility that a few of us *might.* No, I don't expect us to be stamped out by persecution and death, but I must warn you that I am only guessing.)

Anyway, these were the main characteristics of these people. But there is so little known about most of them. All we get generally is a sense, an aroma. Sometimes all that they were allowed to leave us was the sweet smell of their sacrifice. We owe each group so much. We exist today because they existed before us. We gather because of them.

This, then, is the saga of those who seized the banner. And we have asked for the privilege of standing in that triumphant lineage. Remember, though, it is an inheritance of suffering.

One last word about these people.

Incredibly, each one of these groups seemed to have grasped something of the heritage of those who came before them. Turn around and look back. Who do you see first? The ones who stand out the most in the recent past are the Little Flock. But a line can be traced. The Little Flock took the banner from the Brethren. Prior to them we know the Moravians seized the banner from a people called the United Brethren, They in turn got it from the Hussites and the Waldensians. (In case you don't know, that takes us back to about the year 1000!) Before 1000 it is very difficult to gather any information. From 400 A.D. to 1000 A.D. the pages are *almost* blank. But from this we can gain from the record: these groups were always bumping into one another and evolving out of one another.

Every group of any note seems to have turned around; each took the torch from someone who had come before them. We, too, must have such an inheritance. But let's not be narrow. Let's take from *all* of them.

I will close with my second point. Part of our mission is to *look back over church history as well as we can,* perhaps better than anyone has before. Let us study this third force in the Christian family and learn from these people. Learn not from one group, but from all of them, and find all they have to tell us. For this, too, is our mission.

CHAPTER 3

The Witness of the Recent Past

The year was about 1820, the place was Dublin, Ireland. A group of Christians were gathering frequently as a prayer meeting group. But that prayer meeting grew to a home meeting. (That home meeting must have been a very dear experience, but little is known about it.) From a home meeting it grew to a gathering of many Christians, from many places, who joined together in an almost spontaneous exhibition of church life. (This is not too rare; in fact, it happens in all ages. What is rare is if it lasts over four or five years . . . even rarer — almost unheard of — is if it lasts beyond four years *as church life.*) Then, one day in strode a man named John Darby, an Anglican minister. And in a year or two the direction of those dear home meetings was tragically changed! (Shed no tears because the work would have probably died or changed anyway.) The year 1820 was a ripe time in history for the church of Jesus Christ to go through a new stage. It was time for the church to enter the "Bible Study" era. Darby led these Dublin people gradually to the Scripture. (In fact Scripture was only becoming plentiful around the latter part of the 1700's. The stage was set for the ensuing events. By 1830 it was only natural that there be a great deal of interest in the study of the Scripture.)

Darby made the Scripture central in everything for these people. And between the years 1830-1845 there was a golden age of scriptural exposition, perhaps the greatest age of scriptural enlightenment in all of Church history since the first century. But Darby drove his point home *too* well. He said the Scripture must be followed in all things, and he insisted that it be followed the way *he* understood it. I will not recount to you the story of what happened. It is strange that men often end up doing the very opposite of the one thing they stand for so strongly. Darby broke with sound scriptural pattern by pursuing it so hard.

The Plymouth Brethren were not only "Bible Study" centered. They were also an outspoken witness to the body of Christ. (I have to say that as far as I can tell, they did not experience too much of "church life" — precious little, in fact — but *more* than anyone else.) They spoke much about the unity of the body of Christ. And what was the result? Because they took such an inflexible view of everybody believing the Bible exactly the same way, they began to split. They have probably split more than any other Christian movement in the last 1900 years. That is not a criticism. That is a verdict of history.

It's the bittersweet story — the glory and the gore of the Brethren. These people were trying hard! They were completely outside the religious system; they saw great things from the Scripture. And they chopped one another into pieces.

Point: Since religious freedom came in the 1700's, the Christians outside the system have often been as ugly as those *inside*.

Let us go on. Let us look even nearer than the Brethren. The *recent past* history of those outside the system has much to teach us.

We come now to the 1920's and China. Watchman Nee was greatly influenced by the Plymouth Brethren, especially by the Taylorites (whom I must confess were some of the most extreme of all the Brethren). Nee would have nothing to do with the Taylorites themselves, but he learned much from their exposition of Scripture. The work that was raised up by Nee was far more tender, loving and understanding, and I would even say it had far more godliness to it than the Brethren. (Nee gave much emphasis to Christ and to inner experience. It was a *living* faith he presented.) I have little to say about Watchman Nee or the Little Flock. The reason? Too many of that group still live. There is too much that history itself has not yet had time to settle about them. We leave them to the future verdict of Church history. I would say only two things. It has been a long time since they began. In recent years the one greatest single characteristic you would notice of these men, is that most of them are still behind the Bamboo Curtain, suffering greatly. The Little Flock movement is virtually annihilated. They nobly stood in that great witness of the ages; a people worthy of that third stream in Church history. The second thing you would notice among them is a more recent development: the division that is going on between their workers.

Once more, a bittersweet story.

I have told you these stories about the Plymouth Brethren and the Little Flock so you can be concerned. Those living in the recent past — the Brethren and the Little Flock — signal to us the enormous dangers that lie ahead; and the impossibilities of a safe journey. There is carnage everywhere. I have just traced for you, very briefly, that third stream as seen over the last 150 years. We know where the banner stood. It was high, but not high enough. Obviously, there is one thing we must do. We must learn from those who have come before. *And* we will suffer. But suffer what? Let's suffer in a new way. Something others did . . . but not well enough. Let's suffer one another! What is needed is a *people,* and especially workers, who will not divide, who will not split, who will not attack one another, who will not subject the body of Christ to such suffering; men who refuse to divide the body of Christ for any reason.

Perhaps more than anything else, *this* is our mission: to be a counter-witness to the past. The past stop — is *not* good; there is too much division.

But now let's also take a glance at the future: *our* future.

As I gaze into the unknown days ahead of us, I see a great deal of glory, joy, and awe; the awe of watching God work right in our very midst.

But I see suffering ahead. You who dare are going to suffer. Now you are young. You have probably never been deeply hurt. Be sure that suffering, sacrifice, pain (and hurt — deep hurt) are out there waiting for you.

But you know, terms like "sacrifice" are very romantic terms. You can talk to any Christian about this and you can tell immediately that he is willing to "suffer for the Lord." In fact, most Christians who love the Lord are anxiously — romantically — waiting for this encounter.

The Blood Red Pages

This is part of my burden to you. I'm not sure you understand what the word *suffering* means. I think you have one thing in mind and that God has another. There are areas in which Christians never consider that they would ever suffer. For some of you it would never even cross your mind that certain things should be put up with. In fact, once again, we are faced with the annals of Church history. What are the areas in which men *refuse* to suffer? Areas where no one seems to wish to bear the cross. Areas that are "off limits" to suffering. When you look at them, you will realize these are the areas where we *must* learn to suffer. *Here* is our mission.

Shall our *future* be the same as everyone else's *past?*

I am amazed at how many saints in history have been willing to die for Jesus Christ — the ultimate sacrifice. And yet, I am just as amazed that those same dear brothers and sisters who are perfectly willing to die for the Lord, are not willing to stop getting their feelings hurt. Not willing, not able, to get past being upset at little things. That seems so insignificant. Yet the fact is, *this* issue has consistently proven to be more crucial than all the doctrinal debates of Church history combined! "I will not be run over." "I will not be taken advantage of." But most of all . . . we are bound, tied and determined to take a stand for that which is right; to take a stand against *injustice*. Read the record. Christians are determined to speak out for *right* principles. This is an unquestioned, inalienable right. Oh, let the blood flow as high as the horse's bit, let the destruction necessary be the result, but we are going to stand against injustice. We are going to stand for our rights.

Shall our future be as their past?

I'd like you to go back and pick up that history book one more time. First, read the most shameful pages there: the pages where Christians did awful things to one another. Secondly, read the pages where blood ran the reddest. Read the pages of persecution, blood, death. Thirdly, read the pages where men were courageous, where they stood for right principles, where they defended the correct path. Read the pages where men stood for clear, sound, proper teachings.

Now observe something. The pages where Christians fought with one another . . . the pages covered with the most blood of the Lord's people . . . *and* the pages where courageous men stood up for sound doctrine — notice please, *they are all the same pages!* Read it. It's all there. When men stand up for that which is right, against that which is wrong, when men get their feelings hurt because they were taken advantage of, when someone does them wrong, when some other Christian is in error — those are *also* the pages where men die and blood runs deep.

Read the great controversies. Look at the personal charges one man laid against another; see the grudges, the resentments. Then watch the other man do a countercharge. Read what men said in their attacks. Read what other men said in defense against those attacks. Read the messages. Read the fiery denunciation. Look at the pamphlets, piled one on top of another — ugly things, vicious things. Worst of all, this sordid story is found in *every* generation. Unfortunately they are there in every group, in every movement up to *this* very hour.

We not only march in the long lineage of those who have gone on before to do the work of the Lord, but I am sorry to also tell you, we stand in the midst of carnage. If we dare to face the summit, to enter this pageant, we walk a bloody, controversial way. Please note as you walk along how Christians have axed up one another all through the ages.

Look up that mountain side once more. See the banner waving, high and glorious. But that banner is still *not* at the summit. See that banner, but as you do, *also* get your first clear glimpse of what our calling is. (If it is not ours, then it will be someone's.) Somewhere, someday, somehow God must have a people who restrain themselves from being supersensitive. He must have a people who are not peevish, who do not charge. And if charged against, do not countercharge. In fact He is looking for people who are *not* defenders of the faith, *not* standing for principles. He is looking for a people who refuse, at all cost, to engage in bloodletting. He will have such a people. If not us, *someone!*

God is looking for a people who simply will not walk the way of the past. What do I mean? The way that everyone has walked before us. God is looking for a people who will suffer attacks; and even more, a people who *will* suffer the long agonizing consequences of *not* having returned the attack.

This is your Lord's call and you can be certain that He is not going to compromise. He will not lower His standard. Someday He is going to have this people — somewhere, somehow. He is going to wait right where the banner is, until a people come along who will carry that banner to new heights, past this sorry standard of the ages. And what if no one comes along? He will wait! Right there! Your Lord is not going to settle for anything but *His* ways. He will not settle for *our* ways.

24

The Little Man Inside

Is there any hope? The past record shows universal failure. Hope? Frankly we have none. We are bound to fail. Why? Because there is a seed in us — that seed is natural, innate. There is something inalienable written into our very beings; when a man is attacked, he defends. When crossed, he thrusts. "You slander me, and brother, I am going to slander you." Touchy, easily offended, carrying a grudge.

How many Christian workers boast of their bravery . . . in defending themselves, in standing for right principles. It seems to never occur to my breed of people (workers) that this might not be God's highest way. Why? Because such action is innate to our nature. After all, who can denounce bravery?

I would like to talk about this "little fellow" down inside of you. He is a very interesting guy. He is inside of every man and woman. He carries around, pinned on his front vest, a list of principles he lives by, and rights that are undeniably his. Look a little closer at this fellow. Notice that he is filled with opinions . . . about everything. Convictions? Why, he's got convictions running out his ears. He's "a man of *deep convictions.*" And he is not going to compromise any of those lofty convictions either. Hear him articulate his convictions. Watch him pound the desk — "*these* are things that men must *never* compromise on." Furthermore he is ready to wreck anything (and everything) to stand by those convictions.

You have this little man in *you!* He, in turn, has a list of absolutes. That creates a little problem! Why? Unfortunately every one of us has a *different set* of "absolutes." And unfortunately, the lists don't overlap or match. In fact, some of these absolutes are absolutely contrary to one another! Yet each one of these little fellows is an uncompromising little fellow. So, see what you are in for. You can see what the future holds — when you are all grown.

When you are 40 or 50. Each with his absolutes. None of them matching. Wreckage is out there. Wreckage like that which is strewn across the pages of history.

But I'd like to go on a little bit further, talking to you about this little fellow. He must be dealt with. He is master of three areas. First, he can tell you exactly what needs to be done in the daily life of the church. Why, he can tell you the solution to all problems: for instance, what to do with the immoral, what to do with the lazy. He can tell you what to do with the people who don't have jobs, the drunks, the addicts. He can tell you exactly what to do with the cross-eyed and the left-handed. He can show you how to make short work of any church crisis.· He can solve any problem: in your life, in my life . . . in the life of the church, in the life of the workers . . . anybody, anything, anywhere, anytime, under any condition . . . he knows *exactly* what to do.

And he can quote a verse to prove it!

That brings us to the second area he is master of. He is master of the Scripture. This little guy reads the Bible. He can quote you every verse in the Scripture on what to do with *heretics.* He can tell you *what* a heretic is. (By the way, here is his definition: "A heretic is anybody who disagrees with me.") He can tell you the exact scriptural limitations of toleration — when you stop tolerating and when you start chastising. He can give you the seven principles of rebuking another saint. He can hold a workshop on how to *correct* ("in love" . . . of course). He can recite the 10 steps you take on "how to adjust another saint." He can tell you how to mimeograph off the order of worship at an excommunication service. He can tell you the five signs to watch for in order to discern false teaching. In fact, he is paranoid of false teaching. Leave him to his own devices and he will have everybody else in the church paranoid of false teachings. You'll hear him lecture the church on "The Dangers of False Teachings." He'll speak so well that it will cover just about everybody in the church except him! When you leave the lecture, why, you will see a false teaching under every bush. Every time anyone gets up to speak, especially if he is someone that you don't happen to like, lo and behold, there will stand *a false teacher.*

And a false teacher — Aha! When he finishes painting a picture of what a false teacher is, you will see this fang-toothed monster defiling the whole flock. You'll sleep under the bed at night.

This little fellow also knows sound doctrine. He knows the Scripture. He is standing for proper obedience to *all* scriptural injunctions.

But now I want to come to the place where he is truly master. He shines best in telling you what to do with anyone who disagrees with him, especially if they don't teach *his* interpretation of Scripture. And doubly especially if it happens to touch his "pet" doctrine. (Yes, every one has at least one pet doctrine.) And super, super especially on those things in which he has had a *"vision"* from the Lord.

I'd like for you to know this about yourself. Go back and read Church history again. At the same time examine your heart. Then go around and have a talk with different Christian workers across the country.

Listen to them talk. *All* have definite limits of toleration. You can almost hear the "beyond this point I will fight" tone in each one's voice.

By the way, beware of the man who has had a vision from the Lord. He will gladly crucify you if you do not happen to go along with his vision. But now forget others. Look at the little man in *your* heart. Listen to him: "Today, the Lord spoke to me. Today the Lord showed me something out of *His* own heart. And because I am me, and everybody knows I'm the most important character alive today on the stage of Church history, and because it was *God* who spoke to me . . . therefore the thing God spoke to me about must be the *most* important thing in the world." "Stand back. Beware. I've got a vision from God. I'll brook no disagreement."

You're probably more dangerous in the area of a "vision" than you are anywhere else. Men have killed other men because "God spoke to me . . . and the other fellow didn't see it that way." . . . A vision no less! In fact, this is the exact case of what happened to most of the Lord's people who've been put to the torch, to the sword, and to the dungeon.

He knows what to do in all cases. He believes in living by the Scripture in all problem cases. He will tolerate no disagreement.

Beware of one other thing. While he is doing all these things he will speak *so* nobly and sound *so* spiritual.

There is really only one thing this little man can't do! Look at his track record. Oh, he is faithful to the Scripture, there's no question about that; right down to the last drop of blood, he is faithful! But what of his track record *when it comes to suffering?* Look past the noble palaver. He can *inflict,* but he cannot *take.* Look past the scriptural tenets, the mighty convictions, the steely courage. How is this little guy inside of you at *forbearing?* At denying his self nature? At being blind to other men's faults? At putting up with others' weaknesses? How is he at waiting months and years before he corrects, or speaks out? How is he at keeping his mouth utterly closed? Does he have any tolerance, or patience, at all? Can he sit in the middle of a crisis *and do absolutely nothing?* Can he watch the work around him fall to pieces? Can he sit and make no effort to save that work? Can he be quiet when all of his sacred principles are at stake? Can he be still and silent, and watch his life's work crumble before him?

I ask you again, how is this little fellow at going to the cross? The answer is, his record is precious poor. No, it is not poor. It is zero. Don't misjudge that little fellow. He is dangerous. He doesn't suffer the cross, he only quotes Scripture. He only corrects. He only defends. He has wrecked the work of God throughout 1900 years of Church history. He has shamed the name of Jesus Christ. In fact, this little man is the man who lived in the hearts of those Jews and Romans who crucified the Lord Jesus

Christ. He was there during the inquisition, too. He has been present at every controversy in Church history. And never forget, he lives inside of you, *right now.*

What does our future hold? Will our future be as black as the past? Unless we deny that little fellow inside of us, *yes.* And that banner is not going to move.

So I come to my third major point. If we are to go on beyond this present campsite, if we are to press the banner upward, then this little fellow *must* be dealt with.

Most of you are young. You've not yet been in tight places. You've not yet been in church crises. You don't yet know how despicable we workers are. Nor can you imagine how black are our hearts. Your back has not been pressed against the wall. You've not yet lived under unbearable pressure. You've not yet seen a crisis gradually build up and grow until it engulfs you and everyone else in the church. You have not yet walked into that room so charged with tension, there to face the ultimate confrontation.

Those conflagrations are out there in the future. Be sure of it. They're waiting for you. There are some ugly situations with your name on them. And, unfortunately, you will react. Your reaction will be as predictable as the fall. Your reaction will *not* be new. Your reaction will be as old as sin itself. What will you do? Why, the noble thing, of course. The courageous thing. You'll stand up for your convictions. And defend that which is right and stand by "the clear teaching of the Word of God."

That is the open trap. I do not know how long you will live, nor what issues you're going to face . . . but your day will come. And in that day, you will have an airtight case. Be sure, you *will* be right! The other fellow *will* be wrong! Furthermore, you're going to *have* to take action. If you don't, everything you count dear will fall to pieces. The situation will be so critical that unless you speak out, take a firm stand, *everything* will be lost. I repeat: your Scripture will be right. What you'll be doing will be reasonable. What's more, you will be in a position where, if you do not act now, the Kingdom of God will suffer irreparable loss. The present work of God will get off course and the lives of hundreds of people will be affected in a very bad way. The whole future and direction of the work of God on this earth (no, the destiny of the Kingdom itself) hangs in the balance. The stakes will be so high, the principles so important, that probably never in all of Church history has any man had to face what you'll be facing in that moment! And it will be imperative that you act. Now, do me a favor: Just before you act would you turn around and look at history one more time? In every era (and in *every* work) there has been the carnage of those who stood for "the clear teaching of the Scriptures" . . . at the moment of ultimate danger. I beg you: Just take a moment to look. See what happens when men take the situation in hand. See what happens when men cast out that no-good rascal; or correct someone because it is right, logical, reasonable, and above all . . . scriptural. True, it may be all that. But remember this: What you are about to do will also be the most destructive thing — in the whole universe — that you could possibly do to the body of Christ.

Look back one more time through history. This disemboweling of that saint is what everyone in the Roman Catholic stream, in the Protestant stream (and for the last couple hundred years, even in the third stream) has been doing to one another. Obviously it must be *the* thing to do. In fact, as you read those pages you come to the conclusion that men must not have believed there was anything else in the world that could be done. Is this what you will do, too?

Please don't! Because there *is* a better way. A higher way. What?

You can suffer. You can writhe. You can double up in the agony of silence. You can lose. You can be run over. You can be taken advantage of. You can stand by and do nothing while others rip to pieces your life's work. In fact, you can do nothing but stand back and watch while men destroy the present work of God on the earth! Yes, you *can* do that!!! Have you ever thought of such an inconceivable thing?

I call Church history to witness: Where are those who forbear? Where are those who, when attacked, return no fire? Where is that people, where is that man, who will simply sit in the midst of carnage? And though he is armed with every good scriptural reason, where is that man who will do absolutely nothing?

How rare, how very rare are such men. Men, who in the midst of a crisis so paramount that the destruction of the Kingdom is at stake, have chosen to go to the cross . . . and let God's Kingdom fall.

Have you ever known such a man? A man who did nothing during the ultimate hour . . . when the Kingdom itself was at stake; when something absolutely *had* to be done.

I know of one such Man! He walked that rarefied way. And in so ordering His life, He won eternal favor with God. In fact, *He* is the one who set that standard which has been lost. The very standard we now seek to restore!

Seize the banner. Let's plant it at heights Church history has not seen in 1600 years!

But if we are to do this, we must be prepared to *lose.* Everyday we *must* be prepared to lose, to be abused, to be trampled on, and to see our work destroyed. Not once, but again and again . . . while you, in turn, watch in silence as it is being dismembered. If that must be our ultimate lot, so let it be. At least our testimony will be clean.

And can we do such a thing? Probably not. Remember, these are unscaled heights we face. Certainly, we will pay a fearful price, one far greater than those who have invoked their scriptural rights; a people who — finding themselves in those ancient places of dispute — will lay hold of the cross. God is looking for people with divine conduct. Men who, when the very destiny of the heavenly Kingdom is at stake, will silently go to the cross and let everything crumble to pieces. This is not the conduct of earth. This is the conduct of a heavenly new man. And to see such conduct upon this earth once more — this is our mission.

CHAPTER 4

The Solution

Christ.
All we want.
Christ.
All we need.

I want to talk to you about surviving a crisis, or better, *how* to survive a crisis.

Crises Are Inevitable

The day of crisis will come. The church of Jesus Christ will go through fire. You will be there when it comes. That crisis will probably come much sooner than any of you think. What shall you do in that dark hour? Worker, what will you do? Elder, what will you do? The fire will come. But why? To test! To find out what material we're made of: gold or hay. Brother, sister . . . you never dreamed of such discord, backbiting and strife that is possible among the Lord's people . . . It comes. That's not the question. The question is: What will be your conduct in that hour of crisis? Let me repeat, that hour must come. History says it will. Anyone who chooses to go up this mountain path will face the black hours of deep crisis. It is written into the very structure of the universe that these things *must be*. When a crisis first arrives, men will sit down and talk about it. Discussions are held. Some will speak of it being a time to be bold. A time to speak out. And you will look at that hour and know that those men are *right*.

The Problem

But let me ask you, which one among us here is wise enough to know the answer to this question: "When is the right time to act?" Who among us is wise enough to know *which* principle it is that is important enough to be defended? Which brother among us will choose *the* principle which has been violated; *the* right to spill blood over? Who among us will decide what action to take when the "clear teaching of the Word of God" tells us what to do?

I've witnessed many crises and I have noticed that both sides (and they're nearly always diametrically opposed to one another) claim to know exactly what the "clear teaching of the Word of God" is. How will you know which side has the correct interpretation of the "clear Word of God"? As I pointed out, every man on earth has a *different* set of ultimate convictions. Which man's convictions should we follow? You see, that which sets one man off on a tirade doesn't even upset another, whereas the second man feels a blow to all that is holy when yet some other subject is touched. Each one among us has a different length fuse. Each man's threshold of anger is different.

I ask you what *is* a paramount issue?

Was there a greater time in history when men should have spoken out than on the day Jesus Christ was (utterly outside of justice) crucified? Yet, on that day of days, I can name two who did not speak out. God did not. Jesus Christ did not. I ask yet again, *what is* a paramount issue?

Over there sits a brother in the church who will say (no, he will *insist*) that what we need, what the church needs, what has been needed for 1800 years to solve this problem of disunity is for everyone to "be open with one another." He will say, "We have to be honest. We always have to be frank. We always have to be transparent." (And, of course, "We must speak the truth in love.") Is that the solution? Is that the simple solution to 1800 years of disunity? Is the solution *that* simple? Take a look at that brother. By his very nature he is brusk, tenacious, insistent. He isn't really standing for the "clear teaching of the Word of God." He just happens to have a strong, restless soul. He has stated his basic, innate disposition. (Or to put it another way, his fallen nature.) Shall we follow that brother? If we do, we must recognize that sitting over there on the *other* side of the room is still *another* brother. Timid, quiet, reserved. Ask *him* to be frank, transparent and open. Ask him to always speak the truth in love. Wake up! That dear timid soul cannot do that. It would shatter his being. He cannot survive in an atmosphere where everyone is "transparent, open, frank and speaks the truth in love." He will die under such pressure. He cannot live in that atmosphere. One morning he will simply be missing from one of your "honesty sessions."

In fact, if you will come back in a year to two and visit the group that's going to be "honest, frank, open, above board and always speaking the truth in love," you'll find the only people left are those that are honest, frank, strong, abrasive . . . by nature. *Fallen* nature! Give even them enough time and you will come back one day to find only some axe handles, some claws, and some fingernails.

The Solution

We have a problem that is around 1800 years old. Somewhere there must be a solution. Shall we be honest? Perhaps democratic? Diplomatic? Or perhaps we shall continue to follow the greatest war cry of all the ages, "Adhere to the clear teachings of the Word of God!" Yes, let us step over all the dead bodies and do just that.

Unfortunately, strong, steely-willed, opinionated men who burn with strong convictions about "the Word of God" can't get together on that word "clear." Go back to that church history book. Open it on any page. You will see where such a course ended up. It is written in blood, it is written in anguish, in tears. It is written in the suffering of our forefathers.

There must be a standard somewhere. What is it? At just what point *do* you take a stand? What, exactly, will be *our* standard? Is there no north star to guide us?

There sure had better be.

There is! But what?

To answer that all-important question, I'm going to change the subject abruptly.

I'm going to talk to you about lost men, men who are not saved, and ask you a question about evangelism. What do these men need? Our greatly needed *answer* may lie in just such a simple *question!* If you have ever done much witnessing, you have found out it is very difficult to win people to the Lord. I read a lot of books on how to lead people to Christ when I was young. Most of those books told me: "Find out what the lost man's problem is, and answer all of his arguments with 'the clear Word of God.'" The books told me to quote Scripture. *Prove to him he is wrong! From the Bible!* Use the Bible!!!

I did that. And winning people to Christ was monumentally difficult. I opened the Scriptures. I fired point blank. Right between the eyes. As far as I can recall, I never led anybody to Christ that way. And mine is simply the testimony of nearly everyone who has tried that approach to witnessing.

Have you ever had this experience? A lost man will just not get saved if you use the Bible on him in that way. I'm sorry, but it is true.

One day I had a revelation. It was a revelation that was a revolution. And from it I began to be able to lead people to the Lord.

I found out what a lost man needed. I found out what he wanted. It changed my life.

What does a non-Christian want? What, in fact, does he *really* need? Well, you are saved now. *You* know the answer! You know that what he needs is not Scripture proving him wrong. *He needs Christ.* Not only is that what he needs, but that's all he wants. Sometimes he knows that, sometimes he does not. But known or not, all he wants, and all he needs, is Jesus Christ. That was my revelation and my revolution. What do *you* give a lost man when you talk to him? Have you ever tried to give a non-believer anything other than the Lord Jesus Christ? Quote him a dozen Scriptures, if you please. Back him into a corner. Argue with him. Brow beat him. You will end up with nothing to show for it but an abysmal argument.

Try it! Tell him about hell! Describe his lost condition. *Prove* he is wrong. The end will be nothing more than a fuss; that way will not work. Why? Because you are giving him something he does not need and does not want. All his heart wants and all his heart needs is Jesus Christ.

So you give a lost man something besides Christ and what do you end up with? A theological brawl, between a Christian and a non-believer. Well now, if that be true, consider what will happen to you when the man you are talking (arguing) with is a Christian who thinks *he* knows the Scripture!

Now we have a new vantage point. Let's work from it. All the lost man needs, and all the lost man wants, is Christ. That's clear. Then I will ask you another question. What do men who are not lost need?

I believe you can understand if I talk to you this way: let's take your own life. Right now, many of you, at this very moment, are facing a crisis. You have a need, a lack. Right now. What is the solution to your problem? What are you really crying out for? What do *you* need? What do you *want*? Well, for each one of you, the answer is quite different. Or is it? What you really need, and what you really want . . . is Christ. Do you want to know something else? What *I* need is Christ. What *you* want, and what you need ... what I want, and what I need, is the Lord Jesus Christ. Nothing else.

Touch *Him*. . . and *that* is enough!!!

Okay. So much for the individual. What of the church? I have not mentioned the church. Now! What of the church, in crisis? What does the church need? Sometimes you can watch the church go through a dry spell. What does the church need during a dry spell? When a problem arises, what does the church need? What does she want? And when a true life and death struggle arises within the church (or outside the church) (or among the workers), what does the church need *then?*

What does the lost man need? The lost man needs Christ. What does the individual need? He needs Christ. What does he want? Christ. And what do we, as corporate Christians . . . as the church . . . *need?* And what does the church *want?* What does the church *really* want?

For nearly two millenniums, the Lord has been calling His people to the upward heights of that mountain. If we are to complete the work that has begun, it will not be *us* who completes this work. The work will be completed *by Christ Himself.* The work will be completed *in* Christ. The work will be finished *because* of Christ. In other words, Jesus Christ will be central.

The restoration of things lost is very much like *creation!* In creation all things were made by *Him.* Nothing was made that was not made by Him. All things in the whole realm of creation are held together by the Lord Jesus Christ. He is the very unity by which this creation holds together. Christ is the glue of the universe. This universe cannot slip or fragment because of Him.

Without Him it would fly into innumerable pieces. But that is *creation*. What about the church? Well, the church herself *is* the new creation. All must be created by Him; nothing is created that is not by Him, and for Him, and all things hold together *through* Him. When you see this, you will see that the church of Jesus Christ *really* is in great need of restoration. His calling will be accomplished but one way: restoration. But what needs to be restored? Jesus Christ Himself is what needs to be restored. The restoration will be completed when Jesus Christ has been restored, when He is the solution to all things.

What does that mean? " . . . that Christ might have first place in all things." Jesus Christ must first create; secondly, He holds all things together. That Jesus Christ might have first place, yes. But more. That He might have the *only* place. First place where? Everywhere! And in all things! To be sure He must have first place in these areas we are talking about; places where so much of Him is so very needed. And where are these places? He is needed in the individual; in the church. He is needed in the work. He is needed — perhaps more than any other place — between the workers. He is needed between the churches. In me, in you; in my circumstances, in your circumstances; in the work, between the workers; in the church, in the churches; in all these, it will have to be Christ Jesus, and nothing else!

Now we have opened a whole new world. Look up. *That* work is above us. To reach *those* heights you are not going to find any paths. *That* is new territory! Look down on the soil: There are no footprints. Having come this far, we now march off the map! All we have to guide us are the ancient records of men who long ago pioneered this heavenly way.

A moment ago I referred to the circumstances each of you find yourselves in. Some of you are in a very grave mess in your personal lives. That just happens. Christians' lives get messed up from time to time. Nonetheless, regardless of how overwhelming your circumstances may be, I can assure you that your problems pale in comparison to the crises that wait for you all out in the future.

Why? Let me try to explain. As the Lord increases Himself in us, He also increases the scope of His dealing in us. He does this so that He can crush. As He does that He gets what He wants on this earth. As He begins His work in each of you, you can be sure He will leave you gasping. He will put you in tight spots; it is in *those* places He gets out of you what He wants. And He gets *into* you what He wants. I promise you the worst is ahead!

Let's go on. I would like for you to know what you might try as solutions in those hours.

Your first reaction will be wonderment. You will say, "Lord, how shall I handle these things? How should I conduct myself? This is a new trial facing the church; I've never been in anything like this before. What shall I do? Lord, I have nothing to guide me." A personal crisis, a church crisis, a crisis in the work or a crisis among workers. You will cry out, "What shall I do?" – (I can't guarantee you will get any clear answers.)

Well, you can be sure of one thing. At such times the little man inside of you will not lack for a whole bunch of good ideas. Your mind will be popping with good ideas. The hotter the fire, the more good ideas you will have. Those ideas will probably be very similar to the ones that all men for the last 1700 years have had in similar squeezes. Look where *those* good ideas led them! We must break through this fog bank into the higher lands above. *Forget* your good ideas. You can be sure that thousands of men had them before. You know the end result of such ideas.

What will you use then, if you can't employ all those brilliant ideas? *There is a north star.* This is it.

Whatever situation there is out there waiting for you, all you want is the Lord Jesus Christ. All that anyone else really wants is Jesus Christ. All that is needed is Jesus Christ. Tomorrow we face a whole new situation, a new world. It does not matter how dark the hour will get, how unique the situation, how unusual the problem; all that anyone wants, all that anyone really needs and all that is necessary is Jesus Christ. At least this is true for you. Even if it is not true for the other man . . . or for anyone else on the planet.

You must rediscover this fact. You must *restore* this practice. You are going to have to learn a whole new way to walk. "As I face any situation from now on, I must find a way to do only that which is Jesus Christ." No one here today fully understands the total meaning of what I have just said. But hear this, *you must begin.*

In the next few years you are going to find yourself in some hair-raising situations in the church. You are going to face some awful temptations . . . unbelievable temptations. Some of the problems that the church will have to solve will be great. When that hour arrives, recall that lost man. Remember what it was like to try to deal with him when you gave him less than Christ? It did not work. Brother, here is a principle: If dealing with a lost man with something less than Christ does not work . . . then no matter what the circumstances or the situation, no matter how good the solution, or how good it looks . . . *anything less than Christ does not work.* This is true in all of your future. I exhort you, as you face your predicaments, DO NOT MOVE until you have gotten Christ, *and only Christ.* Christ is the solution. He *is* the working out. Less than Christ does *not* work. It never has, and never will. Sit until you know you have laid hold of Christ; do nothing. And when you have laid hold of Christ, do nothing *else.* Until you have Christ and only Christ, and until you can impart nothing but Christ and only Christ, sit there and let everything fall to pieces.

This is our call.

I would like to talk a little now about how to get ready for those inevitable days that lie ahead. It may come to you individually, or it may happen to us all, corporately, as the church. Whatever it is, it will be worse than you could ever believe right now. Your first reaction will be, "Find a solution!" "Work it out!" Let me warn you, when that day comes, you had better have already acquired a great deal of experience in taking Christ in your daily situations.

You need to know Him as your everything *now,* in the little daily problems, so that you can locate Him in these gigantic encounters.

So begin! Later when the ultimate trial comes, you will have some experience to draw from. What is needed? Christ. What is wanted? Christ. What will not work? Anything that is not Christ.

We've talked about what the *lost* need, we've seen what *you* need. Let's see what *others* need.

Let's say that a brother talks to you, seeking your counsel. If you give him less than Christ, you have not met his need. If you give him an opinion, you will give him something that *will* help. Though he has been given some help, in fact, you have really damaged him. You have given him something short of Christ. Somewhere, somehow, in every situation, you are going to have to find Christ to give him. You must find Christ, and impart Christ and impart nothing but Christ.

When you yourself get into an awful crisis, your first reaction is going to be, "I want out of here." If you find a way out, you have not solved your problem, you have gotten around your problem. You have not found a solution. You have simply gotten *around* finding a solution. Other Christians in the fire are the same way. They automatically want, first and foremost, *out.* "I want relief!" So for all of us, if I try to help another believer with something other than Christ, if I try to speak something besides Christ, if I try to do something besides Christ, if I try to work out a solution that is not Christ, I will suffer loss. So will he.

I speak of a lofty goal. Can we possibly scale such heights? Quite frankly we cannot. The heights are too steep. To expect to average 100% perfection in a situation such as this is simply demanding too much of fallen man. So, the church must be a place where getting "less than Christ" can be survived occasionally. The only way that can happen is that "less than Christ" be the rare exception. (This is why the Lord has given each of us *seventy* years to live on this earth. During that seventy years you are bound to suffer some reverses. In fact, a whole bunch of them.) You are bound to miss the mark, and — praise God — learn some valuable lessons. When it comes to learning Christ and giving Christ, we are going to make some C's and D's before we start making B's and A's. (We will probably start this class making F's.) Your first report card may not look too good. If such is the case, I trust the Lord will not write "Ichabod" on you, on us. But saints, we can not make a habit of low grades. The church can survive that for a little while, but not long. You cannot survive a steady diet of less than Christ. So we must begin. Here. Today. We must begin to allow the Lord to work Himself into us in every way, and in every crisis and in every problem. Beyond that we must begin to open ourselves to the cross. The cross *must* be applied to *everything* which is less than Christ.

So let's start preparing ourselves for the inevitable. Start getting *this* kind of experience. The church must rise above its present level. We must go beyond this place, *beyond* where the Lord has brought us thus far. We will only go beyond this present point as we begin to know Him, and *take Him* in all things.

Now I must get a little more practical. What do I mean by knowing only Christ? Certainly I am not speaking of something religious. I am not asking you, when you get into a crisis, to ask that insipid, religious question, "What would Jesus do if He were in my place?" That is a bunch of religious rot; pure bondage. What, then, did I mean, "taking Christ and giving nothing but Christ"? I mean when you have gotten past every human motive, and everything has been purged out of you — when the hidden motives of the heart have been dealt with — and you know that there is nothing coming from you but the living Lord. (In fact, it is the Lord's life that is living and reigning.) Everything, every motive in your heart has been tried, every hope has gone to the cross, every good idea you have had has been crucified, and deep in the depths of your being there have welled up the springs of God Himself. He has now become the One who is living and speaking. Not until then. Not until *then*.

You might say there is point A, point B and point C. Point A is where the crisis begins. Point B is when you get all the ideas. (Point B is where you have a lot of human reactions, good ideas for solutions . . . and it is *here* that most men in Church history have taken action.)

You can't always prevent point B from happening . . . but you can take it to the cross. May He be praised . . . there is a point C. Point C is when you have found the Lord *and you know it.* Such a place is possible! Everything else has been purged away. Point B was annihilated, swept away by God. Now you have come to the point where you're willing to lose *all.* You have the mind of the Lord; you can speak. (No! That is not accurate. Often you will know that you *cannot* speak. To speak would be less than the Lord. All you can do — most likely — is be silent. Go to the cross. And die.) All I want you to know is this: Between point A and point C there will have to be a great deal of suffering, heartache and agony. Pure agony!

Let's review. I need Christ. You need Christ. A non-Christian needs Christ. The church needs Christ. Your brother with a problem needs Christ. That leaves one person: the worker.

I have asked you to read Church history. Now, may I suggest you also read carefully the record left us in Acts. If you do you will notice a series of problems. Some between members. Some between individuals. Some between churches and some between workers. The first big church problem that ever developed was in Jerusalem. It was local, and the problem was not caused by workers. Widows and food were the issue. But notice the next big problem. It happened at Antioch. *This* problem was brought on by workers from Jerusalem. Most really serious problems are brought on by workers. The problem was so big that a Jerusalem council was called. Many conflicts followed after that, but you can be sure that in every case there were at least a few men present who were willing to endure almost superhuman suffering. They did so for the sake of the unity of the body. That was a hallmark of the early believers.

44

You don't find such a nice record *after* the first century. I would like to also point out that most problems, most controversies, which have arisen since 325 have *not* even been scriptural problems. They were over things like...well...church buildings (which is not a scriptural problem). Let's hope that most of our problems will at least be scriptural; problems that are true duplicates of problems found in *church life* of the early saints. If we follow the Lord's way, they will be.

Suffice it to say that as you read the record beyond 300 A.D., the workers have caused most of the conflicts. And now *we* must walk into the arena of church history. How high a standard we must establish. Now. Otherwise we are lost.

Most of you are young now but you will not always be that way. You will get older, and some of you will be gifted by the Lord. Some of you will enter into the work of the Lord. Well, saints, you had better start taking Christ as your everything now. You had better get to know this thing called "loss" and "denial." If you wait until you're a worker to *start* living such a life, you have waited too long. (And if you, dear reader, are a worker, whoever you are . . . the wisest thing you can do is turn in your badge. Start all over again. You're a dangerous commodity. Workers today know neither church life, denial, nor the deep things of God. The age we live in did *not* properly prepare you for the Lord's work.) The Lord will give you an introduction to this higher walk in little things, like learning to live with your roommate! He is faithful to send the little crises every day. Later He will increase the crises. The demand for loss gets bigger! Will your take Christ in the small problem? You had better! You'll need a great deal of practice for the titanic encounters which lie ahead. Be sure: if you get a great deal of practice in taking Christ as your all now, you can expect that later on -- when it comes to dealing with the work and the worker -- you will need every bit of that experience to draw from. The situations are grave, Himalayan! Each rung is not only a little higher, but a little harder. Each time the stakes are

45

greater. Each time the possibility of failure is greater; each time the demand that you lose calls for a *greater* loss! Unfortunately, the temptation to settle for less than Christ also gets greater. The temptation to pick up a tool unworthy of the Lord's name grows with every succeeding year. Yes, you need a lot of practice. NOW. So begin now.

Do you need some motivation to be willing to experience such a hard calling? Look up: see the prospects. Consider the new things that God could have upon earth. Learn to lose. Learn to suffer. Learn while you're simple, uncomplicated. Lay in your life a foundation of suffering, pain and loss . . . now!

Let me press the point. What will happen if you *don't?!* Well, you're going to go through some soul-searching, spirit-crushing experiences. And what happens in those hours if you act with less than Christ? You will have reverted to those ways which men have employed for 1700 years! Be very certain of that. There *are* other ways. Unfortunately, some of these ways are very high . . . very spiritual and noble. In fact, scriptural! Most of all they are *extremely* reasonable. Your mind will be overwhelmed by how *rational* this course is. You *will have* an excuse. You will have a verse to justify your actions!

I'm not sure you understand. There are tools. Good ones. But they are less than Christ.

One day you *must* discern the difference between what is good, but less than Christ . . . and what is Christ. You must have strong spirits. *You need* experience! The experience you must have, though, can only be seen by one *hanging* on a cross. Things look different there than anyplace else on earth. Let me explain what I mean. You're blind until you can see things from the cross. There are some things that can only be seen by one suspended in crucifixion: things you will never know, things you will never see, 'til you can see while nailed between heaven and earth. The Lord *must* put every one of His servants through these experiences. He *must* put you on the cross. Some experiences awaiting you are downright horrible. No man can possibly endure them unless he has had some "just slightly less severe" and similar experiences just a short time previously. Why? Without such pre-conditioning you will be destroyed!

Many of you want to be a worker. I can't give you one clear definition of the job qualifications (forgive me for being facetious), but I can tell you of some excellent preparation. In fact, I will list *essential* preparation. *Essential* if the man is to be what God wishes him to be. Preparation to be a worker: the *frequent* experience of being nailed to a cross. The frequent experience of losing everything. I repeat, there are things you learn in these straits that you learn nowhere else.

What shall you see as you hang from the cross? One thing: regardless of the darkness of the hour, the seriousness of the conflict, or the greatness of the stakes, all you need is Christ. Even on the cross! In everything it must be Christ. Even your conduct during a crucifixion! *Your* crucifixion! Never forget that.

So, we have found the mark. Now, look up that mountain slope. See! There! The heights! These we must now scale. May God have a people on the earth who are a people of the cross; a people of Christ and only Christ.

May this, oh Lord, be our mission.

CHAPTER 5

Surviving the Aftermath

We have talked about crises; about bloody days ahead. We have talked about what to do in those days. Our conduct. The solution. (The solution being to know nothing but Christ.) What about when the crisis is past, when the whole ordeal is over? Now you face a day as critical as the crisis. A crisis always witnesses the falling away of many people. Men get destroyed in crises. But oddly enough there is another period of destruction . . . equally as great. Many who make it through a crisis are destroyed by the aftermath. Let's say a day comes when you see impending strife. You lay down your life. You do not attack. You do not react when attacked. You do not claim your scriptural rights. You do nothing. What will be the result?

Some of you might feel, "Well, the Lord will step in and deliver me." This may be. I doubt it. If He does, you can be sure it will be the exception. I don't think you can imagine just how dark the nights will be; how long until sunrise. Most of you cannot believe how charged with suffering will be your scroll. You *will be* run over. You will be denounced. Slandered. In fact: crucified. This will be your lot. And furthermore, there will be no one around noticing how noble you were during the ordeal. In fact, you will be attacked for being silent. It is a situation of . . . hanged if you do . . . hanged if you don't. The fairest, noblest conduct will not only *not* be noticed . . . it will be assaulted. And while all that is going on, your life will be crushed. Your dreams shattered. Your work decimated. Your ministry destroyed. Your reputation ruined. You probably will be back to zero, or close to it.

Aftermaths Also Ruin

That brings us to the next point. When it is over, when you come out, with your garments smoking, your soul crushed and your spirit no longer functioning . . . what then? (I'm talking about church crises, inter-church crises and conflicts between workers, as well as some of the mammoth personal problems that come our way.)

I think I can tell you exactly what will happen to you, based on what has happened to most people who go through these ordeals, these tragic, horrible upheavals. You can expect that you will be shipwrecked for the rest of your life! That's it! Spiritually destroyed. Mesmerized. Bitter. Walking, dazed, down misty corridors. Forever haunted by the memories of those ghastly hours. *Beyond repair!*

Will that be your end? Is that the only possible end for you? For men who allow the loss of all things? Probably. But there should be a better something than that. Why? Because you *are* going to go through these horrendous trials! Most people who go through them *never* survive. Yet there must be some means of survival. Praise the Lord, there is. But it is on further up the hill . . . quite a ways.

You had better know that way. You'd better live by it. *Here* is your only hope! How to survive the aftermath of a crucifixion is one of the most important things you'll ever learn.

Your Past

Most of you are young. You have not yet gone through the deep crises of which I have spoken. But on the other hand, I think every

50

one of you has been disappointed, haven't you? Keenly hurt? Disappointments can ruin you. So let me ask you ... think back ... how did you conduct yourself when you went through the darkest hour you have ever lived? The answer will give you some clue as to how you are going to fare in future crises.

So many of you are young. I'm grateful for this, for many reasons. One of them is because you do not have a great deal of *past*. Mark that word. It is to this that I want to address myself: the past. If you are to survive the ordeals that I have described, then you must never collect a past! May God be merciful to you that you never have a past.

Now what do I mean by such a term? Well, along the years you have many experiences — some positive, some very negative. A few almost destroy you. Some will be so damaging it's unbelievable. The younger you are, the fewer of these experiences you've had. Yet every one of you have had a past. Enough to appreciate what I am saying: a bad experience can wreck you.

I have seen a large number of men wrecked by what happened to them. They were wrecked because of *one* thing. They could never shake loose of the dreadful experience. It dogged them; it preyed on them day and night. Somewhere they were hurt by someone. Until this very day they just cannot recover from it. The memory is there. It gnaws at their hearts. Call it the dark, unshakeable memory!

Do you know who it will be who'll play the greatest role in giving you a past? Well, it could be an employer. It may be someone kin to you. But do you know who it's *most likely* to be? A Christian. Unbelievable as it seems, no one can hurt you quite as deeply as a Christian. They will author most of your dreadful memories. Once more, this is a record of Church history. (Chances are it will be a worker who does it.) This is true. Don't be surprised if it happens *to you*.

There's a very heavy verse of Scripture in Hebrews. Through one of His writers the Lord says, "Be careful that a root of bitterness does not grow up in you." That remains true even if it is a Christian who hurts you and causes the bitterness.

I've seen a lot of men taken out of the race. Except for (perhaps?) immorality and outright heresy, the thing that has destroyed most men has been rebellion and *bitterness. Bitterness!* It destroys more Christians than just about any other obstacle that is placed before us in this race we are destined to run.

What is bitterness? When can you know it has you? You may know that bitterness has come into your life when you drag your past around. Once you have drug your *past* into your *present,* bitterness spreads into your soul like a cankerworm. Soon that bitterness will infect not only you but all those around you. You will infect them. You're destroyed, and now you're destroying others.

I want to repeat myself. There's trouble ahead *for you!* There's no escaping it. If any of you think that someone has hurt you up until now you haven't seen anything yet. It would be wiser if you packed your bag today and left and never returned . . . and save yourself from the anguish ahead. I'm speaking from a scriptural viewpoint, *and* I am speaking from experience—there's trouble ahead.

We have to take a stand on this subject. After all, the world, and everything that's in this world, is going to rise up and assault us one of these days. If you allow your past into your present . . . if you should *not* allow Christ to be your past . . . then your future will destroy you. You cannot possibly survive the future if there is a root of bitterness in your present. The root of bitterness destroys every man it touches. I am telling you; do not let yesterday into your today. There is only one thing you should allow into your today. That is Christ, and only Christ. Christ is the only way through the crises that lie ahead.

(I am trying to tell you how to get beyond the aftermath of a cruci-fixion.)

What do I mean by," never acquire a past?" Is it not true that all of us have a past? No, it is not true. We only have a past *if* we drag our dark experiences into our present life. How can you prevent that? By knowing only the Lord Jesus in your present. You see, the Lord Jesus is not past. He is not present. He is not future. He is outside time and space. He covers the dark memories. Make experience of Him *your* present. There is hope for survival in that.

Maybe I should define what I mean by "the past." Simply stated, the past is a bad experience. By that definition, everyone in this room has a past, true. But if you are to go on, upward, your past will have to end *today*. Your past will have to be the Lord. Otherwise you are going to be destroyed. The dark memories must be laid aside.

Let me give an illustration: You know that a few days ago I returned from a trip to mid-America. How was my trip? Pleasant, thank you! I was there for about a week. Was I hurt by anything happened there? Not at all! In fact, the trip home was wonderful. As I look over yester-day, I see only Christ. Now what if I talked to you about the day before yesterday? I can say it was a wonderful day, too. In fact, all I recall about that day is Christ. You should have been there. But what about the day before? Well, if probed back in my calendar long enough you just might run across a day that was not so hot. There was a day that was not Christ. The things in it were ugly. What am I going to do with that awful day I had? Well, if I choose, I can make that day part of my present. I can think about that day. I can talk about that day. To anyone. To everyone. I can analyze that day. I can justify that day. I can relive that day. I can nourish that day. I can take that day home with me; I can adopt it! I can feed it! I can give it a bedroom! I can make it a permanent part of my life. I can establish that day as part of my past history. I can talk about it and remember it. And be sure: if a day is bad enough, a situation grizzly enough, that's exactly what will happen.

Did I really have a day *that* bad? Well, brothers, *that depends*. If I allow it to be, yes . . . it might well have been a very horrible day. There might be some days in my past experience, if I allow them into my life today, to dwell there, that can destroy me. I could look back and say, "That was the worst day I ever lived. This thing that happened was unfair, I was mistreated, those were a bunch of good-for-nothing people who did that," etc., etc. If I take *that* viewpoint, if I yield to that conduct, then . . . yes, I've had some horrible experiences in my life . . . days that wrecked my life. The fact is, I could make a career out of what happened to me one day. Have you ever had a day in your life like that? One so unjust that it could destroy you, that haunts you, that you could pitch a tent and make it your career? You could talk about it, dwell on it, nurture it for the rest of your life. Have you ever been *that* deeply hurt? Have you ever had something so abysmal happen you could write a book about it? Even *three* books! Have you ever had a day you could launch a monthly magazine just to crusade against those involved? Have you ever had a day so bad that you could launch a nationwide movement just to stop the dirty rascals? Well, that's the kind of day that can get deep down in your soul, make its home there, *and destroy you.* In fact, that's exactly what happens to many men.

Have I ever had a day like that? The answer is: *only* if I bring it home and put it to bed.

There are some days so horrible, so unfair, that when they happen, many of the Lord's people simply never recover from them. If I ever happen to have a day like that, and if I do not shake that day, then it will follow me into my present, and then it is no longer my terrible past. It is my bitter present. I am damaged. If something does not happen quickly, if it gets into my inner man, and thereby in my future, then I am ruined! *You are going to have such days!* I can see them already on the horizon. Or, I should say, "Look up, there they are!" They're waiting for you up there, somewhere on the slope of that mountain! They are awaiting the pilgrim who dares venture the heights.

Are you sure you still want to make this trip? If so, then what is past must be laid aside. Out there in the future, when you run into bad days, those days must be laid aside immediately. You must lay them aside.

You must not allow one bit of your past into your present, nor into your future. It is past; it is certainly not Christ. Therefore it *is* gone! And, praise God, it *is* forgotten. That day has been replaced. Glory.

In fact, I can't quite remember that day. What did happen? I'm sorry, I don't remember. It is gone! Was that last week, or did it happen last year; what was the date, was it fair or unfair? I'm sorry, I cannot recall. It never made a home in my heart.

Well, have you been curious about some of the things that have taken place in my past?

Do you really want to know what has happened to me in crisis days? (Yes, you do! Fallen man has the curiosity of a cat.) What are some of my past experiences?

Well, I could probably tell you stories that would smoke your ears! But look at me! Anyone my age has had lots of things happen to him. And, unfortunately, some men dwell on those events and talk about them for years. Be careful, when you have lived another twenty years. Unpleasant experiences will have filled a good part of your life. But they're not so remarkable. A lot of the Lord's servants have had horrible experiences. Other men rarely know about them, though. Why? Because they never talk about them; consequently, the bloody days are soon forgotten. Yet another man may talk about such things all the rest of his life. The bad experiences have made home in his heart.

By the way, when you go through these dark days there will probably be some other saints going through them, too. Be careful: you will want to get together and form a "bitterness club." People in deep trouble magnetize one another. You can stand around and talk to one another about what happened, over and over, for the rest of your lives. Better *you* pack your bags and leave town. If you cannot shake the thing, at least don't dwell among those who are forever damaged by it. Soon their hurt is your hurt and your hurt is their hurt. Soon your view is their view, their view yours. Their damage your damage, your prejudice their prejudice. Much harm will come to you, brother. Not only will you be hurt but you have hurt so many others . . . "lest it take root in others' hearts."

Frankly, I have just given a case history of *Church* history. Here it is in a nutshell: Someone got hurt; he lashed out at the person who hurt him. Then others took offense at being fired on and they returned the fire. Maybe what was said was unfair, but the fire they returned was also unfair. Sure, their lawful right had been massacred, their reputation ruined and what was said of them was just not the thing to do. But when it was over with, many men on both sides were ruined forever. None went to the cross.

Such conduct is not Christ. Therefore, you do not dare pass such conduct on to anyone. Maybe you feel you are justified in being hurt. Okay. You may even feel justified in speaking out. Perhaps you are, but what you are about to say is not Christ, and when you say it — it is going to ruin *others*.

Here is what I am saying to you all: It is time that Church history had a better page inserted into it. All of the past must stop here, today, with us.

If you allow a deep hurt to find its place in your life, then the banner will not move. If the banner moves it will move only because God has a group of people who have given up the privilege of having a past. There must be a people on this earth who are blind to their own rights — a people blind to what others say, and a people who do not answer, in kind, the unfair treatment they have received.

56

If that banner moves, it will be because the past has ceased to exist. That means that every negative thing that has ever happened to you . . . never happened.

Curiosity

A moment ago I referred to man's curiosity. Well, even your curiosity is going to have to become the Lord Jesus Christ. We humans are a curious people. We get wind that something's happening . . . and especially if we hear it's something negative . . . we immediately want to know *all* about it! Look. Here comes a whole flock of people. Now they are standing in front of your door anxiously waiting for you to influence them. You can almost hear them say, "Prejudice me!" "Oh, color my viewpoint." "Oh, quick, quick, tell me the ugly story. I'll be on your side. Just fill in the details so I can be appropriately aghast! I can hardly wait! Tell me the grizzly details. Whatever they are, I promise to side with your version of the whole smelly thing!"

The world's full of this kind. In fact you may be one of them! Probably are! Saints, not only do you lay down your past, but you do not spread it around to others. You do not assuage someone else's insatiable curiosity.

(All of this calls for a totally new lifestyle — a new way to think, act, live. A way of life contrary to your cultural habits and contrary to your old man.)

Your curiosity will have to go. Refrain from knowing the sordid things that others have gone through. Yes, it may be fun to hear. Yes, it may be terribly interesting! Yes, it may be entertaining! Yes, it will satisfy your old man . . . like birthday cake satisifes a little boy! But still you ought not hear, and still you ought not speak. I doubt that you could find a more pleasant way to spend this evening than listening to some sordid Christian mess. And tomorrow! And Tomorrow! You can make it the main topic of conversation among all your Christian friends. Listen, the ears of the Lord's people were not created for such things. We ought not to ever hear about the poor conduct of the Lord's people. Leave it to be read in the history books! Perhaps if we read what happened a hundred or two hundred years ago we might learn a lesson. But to talk about what is current brings darkness into our own souls. If we allow ourselves such a neat treat, we pay an awful price for the entertainment. Why? Because we've become exactly like those who walked before us. Exactly! For *this* is what they did. And we will leave the same wreckage behind us that they did. Fun, yes. Entertaining, yes. What everyone has done before us, yes. But is it Christ? No.

And if it is not Christ? Then it is a luxury we cannot afford.

Church problems, workers' problems, individuals' problems ... all are interesting, entertaining and all satisfy your curiosity. But the awful conflicts are not worthy of the Lord in their being repeated. In satisfying your curiosity you have also sacrificed the position of that banner! You may have your curiosity wined and dined for the evening, you may have gained a lot of interesting stories to pass on to other curious people, but, oh, oh, the cost you pay. Oh, the destruction that you have wrought. (You can rationalize and say, "I only told them so they wouldn't fall into the same error." Yes, you may help that person and it may be therapeutic to your wounded feelings to speak about it. I admit it could even conceivably be helpful. But mark this, *it is not necessary*. Ever! There is only one thing that is necessary, and that is Christ.)

I said it before, I say again: where are a people willing to suffer?

I give you good news: we do not have to speak about our past. You are not compelled to damage others by the experience you went through. Oh, you can! But you don't have to! You can drop your past. All any of us really need is Christ. And I don't care how curious the brother in front of you may act, nor how he begs to hear the story, remember all that *he really wants* is the Lord. Give him the Lord. That's all he *needs*. Somewhere down inside of you, hoping against hope, is another person. And somewhere deep inside your fellow Christian, hoping against hope, is *another* man. *That* man is hoping that he will hear nothing but Christ from you; and if that man does get Christ from you he will be edified, and he will be strengthened and perhaps, just perhaps, he will be changed for the rest of his life. He may learn a lesson in conduct that changes his direction forever.

Tools You Must Not Use

Let me tell you a secret, a secret you *will* learn someday. Once you discover this secret, you'll be tempted, as most of us are, to use this secret.

Here it is: you can use your past as a tool for your own advantage. What do I mean by such a statement? You can use your past to unify the work. (*Your* work.) All those grizzly experiences you went through. Remember? You can use them to warn people against *other* folk. In so doing you will unify them around a common prejudice. This is one of the great secrets of launching and sustaining a movement! Someone once said, if you want to start a movement then get a group of people together and teach them how to hate a common enemy. And it is true. That fact needs exposing.

Let me illustrate. One day you were hurt by someone else; then you got bitter. Or maybe it's not that at all. Perhaps your work is being threatened by someone in your group. Okay. You have a problem. You begin looking around for a tool to save the hour. Actually, all you need is one good illustration. You see the present danger. Now, reach into your past and pull out an experience that will illustrate this *present* danger. Make it one that will cause everybody's hair to stand on their necks. A real blood chiller. The more terrifying, the better. Many Christian workers have built their whole life's work on the basis of telling stories about their enemies. By prejudicing their followers they rally everyone around a common enemy, or a common fear. Look around you. Most Christian work today is held together by being taught either to hate or to fear someone or something. Either that, or some single-shot vision (or *both*, combined). It is not Christ that unifies most groups. It is often a common enemy. Will you use your past as such a tool? Listen, dear saint of the Lord. *You do not have any enemies.* Remember that! As long as you live, you have no enemies! You have only one thing, and that is the Lord.

You will find, the longer you live, that there are many tools lying around for you to pick up. In a few years all of you will have several dozen of them, and you would really get a charge out of picking up a few of them. Some of those tools are perfect to get you through a crisis. A crisis that is threatening *your* position. With that one tool you could step forward and unify . . . you could step forward and banish . . . the impending threat. The longer you live the more tools there will be. Some of them look very noble. Look again. Everyone of them is *less* than Christ!

I'm sorry to say the tools don't go away, either. At times you will feel you absolutely cannot perform the task God has called you to unless you pick up one of these tools. You know full well that unless you pick them up *all of your work will be lost.* (After all, the little imp inside says, "You went through that simply awful experience just a few years ago. It's just like this one. Go ahead. Warn everyone. And do a job so good it will scare everybody stone blind . . . and save you in this present threat.) Then let your work be lost. All the Lord's people need is Christ. If Jesus Christ will not suffice, if Christ cannot deliver you out of the situation you are in, then let everything go to destruction.

How then shall I deal with my past? By leaving it. There is only one experience out of my past that I need to bring into my present, all the rest *I leave.* All that I need to carry into the future is Christ. The Christ whom I have experienced. If I speak of anything other than Christ, or that is not Christ, I've brought something into my present and I'm in a risky place. If I cannot get all the way from A to C (with B totally washed away), then I ought never try to speak the Word. If you cannot get to point C, say nothing. If necessary, pack and leave.

During the few years that I have lived on this earth, I have picked up just a little bit of Christ. Praise the Lord. I can carry *that* with me out of my past, but nothing else. If I do anything, or say anything out of my past that is not Christ, I've fallen short. Take what you have of Christ into the future.

The things we're dealing with here are not quickly grasped, but I believe we can learn these lessons. I must have a past that is Christ, or I must have no past at all. Such a standard can be reached. We *can* make it.

Your Present

We just talked about going through the cross. Now we're going to look at how to survive the aftermath of a crisis. We have talked about the past, now let's look at the present. The present is brand new. It is a world that has not yet been experienced.

Let's say that you have gone through a horrible nightmare. And let's also imagine that you have someway shaken loose from it. You're not living in the past, you're strictly in the present. Lo and behold . . . just as you begin to embark on a new experience, you run into the cross again! When that happens, what will you want? The same thing you wanted in the past. Out! Remember the little man down inside? He can still supply you with all the ways out. And he is still opposed to going to the cross. (He has answers, but remember he is basically dishonest. In fact, he is a crook.) Furthermore, that little man is a sissy. He will cook up new ways for you to escape the cross of the present.

Right now you're young. In a way, this is the easiest time of your life to be a Christian. You are in the church, not yet married. Your roommate offends you. You face a black and white decision. Would that all your future experiences with the cross could be so black and white. Yours is a simple decision: sulk, or go to the cross! When you get older, these blacks and whites fade; they become pastels. As this happens you discover it is much more difficult to recognize that little crook inside you. The problem becomes greater, the stakes become higher, the issues more cataclysmic, but the shades dim. Boundaries fade. Pastels. You are in rarefied air. You will ask yourself, "What is the right way?" In that day it will honestly be hard for you to know the answer.

Be warned. That little crook *will* be right there. Even as you are old, he will be saying, "If ever there was a time to speak out, now is that time." Here is what I would like to leave you with. Regardless of the issues, just remember . . . that little man, with all of his ideas, *is not the Lord.* He *is not* the Lord. You need present experience, in current circumstances, to distinguish between the little crook and the Lord.

Now I know what your question is. "Gene, are we going to let people run all over us for the rest of our lives, then?" That's a good question. Shall we become a passive people, introspective, weak-willed, afraid to speak, afraid to move forward? Will we become like the old saying, "a mild-mannered people being urged on by a mild-mannered man, to become more mild-mannered"?

Let's ask the Lord to make us strong. Bold and fearless. Did you know that there's nothing any stronger, or more fearless (or more to be feared), than a courageous man who is willing to be crucified? The mightiest man that ever lived was the man who was willing to go to the cross.

We are going to be strong and fearless. But there's nothing more powerful on this earth than a man who can bridle his strength, sit down and . . . wait. A man who can do nothing in the midst of a world that is melting; that is the highest order of strength. That is *divine* strength. No higher point has ever been reached in manhood or bravery than by that man who quietly submits to the unjust, unjustified crucifixion. That fact was proven 2000 years ago.

But will this not open us to error, always giving in to the wrong? And also, if things go wrong in the church . . . and all the fine people yield . . . who will stop the wrong element? Who will keep all of us from veering off course? Who will speak out against all the unjust things? Who will bring us back when some heretic among us tries to lead us off into error?

These are good questions. Men have asked them for centuries. In fact, these questions sound absolutely crucial — and unanswerable. But I also want you to know that throughout history men have come up with only *one* answer! "We must be defenders of the faith." In the dark hours, *speak out!*

These questions have been asked before, for ages; and men have also come up with the same answer for ages. And while all these high-principled people are living by all these high-sounding principles, the Lord's work on the earth has been cut to ribbons.

Today the Lord is looking for a group of people who will say, "We will know nothing but the Lord. Someway, Lord, You will have to keep us on course, even in the midst of the most fearsome hour we will ever live."

This, then, is how we must face our daily present.

The Hornets of God

I know it may sound immature and even adolescent to suggest that we move in such a direction. But let me tell you a story. You are all familiar with Moses taking about one million people and leaving Egypt. They were headed for the promised land. Finally, after nearly forty years, they got to the border of the land promised. But do you know, that was the *second* time they got to the border? The *second* time they were almost ready to go in? Back when they first left Egypt, they came almost immediately to the border of the promised land. But they never went in. Do you know why? The Lord had told them to go in. Remember? They sent in twelve spies. They began asking questions. "How are we going to take the land with all those people already in there? They are our enemies, Lord. They are committed to our destruction. How can we possibly survive the odds?"

For Israel this was a crucial hour. The Lord had an interesting answer. He simply said, "Go in and I will drive your enemies out before you." They refused to believe Him.

By the way, the Lord explained, in the book of Exodus (23:28), exactly how He, Himself would drive out all of the enemies who lived in the land.

Men would not even have had to fight!!! Then how? God said, "There will be hornets." The Lord was not going to use human strength. He was going to let the people walk into the face of certain defeat, and then He was sovereignly going to deliver them. This was God's highest way. Some 38 or 40 years later when they went into the land, God made them fight every inch of the way because their fathers before them had not trusted the Lord. They had not trusted the hornets of God.

The Lord told them how it would be. "As you advance, one city at a time, as you need the room, as they come out to meet you, I will send hornets. But I will do it only as you advance. I will do it only as you need room. I will not hand you a land totally conquered. If I did that, the land would be vacant. I will *not* give you one great, sweeping victory." The Lord had planned to drive out the enemy by hornets as the people needed the land. The hornets would come and drive out the enemy during the crises. They didn't believe. It was too simple a solution to too big a problem. They were too mature, too discerning, too full of wisdom. Nearly forty years later, God had to call on the young. Only kids believe in hornets!

Men had been called on to trust the hornets. God had intended to do all the fighting. That is the highest way.

I'm aware that that's not a very sensible answer to your questions. Who will keep us from being led off by some heretic? I don't know. Who will keep the work from being destroyed? I don't know. Maybe it will be destroyed! No man should do anything to destroy it. No man should do anything to save it. But what if someone does do something to destroy it? Then you should do nothing to save it. When the smoke clears, what will be left will be stone. What is burned is wood, hay and stubble. God only builds with fireproof material. So let the fire come. Stone and gold don't burn up in fire; not even in a holocaust.

Frankly, I would rather lose *this* way than *win* the other way. Be the man who can be defeated. Be the man who can lose. Be the man who can see a life's work destroyed. Someway God will keep us, or someway He will bring out from an already infinitesimally small work, yet a smaller work of overcomers. When you are attacked against all reason, against all odds . . . *trust the hornets of God*. If you cannot be delivered this way, *then be destroyed*. At all cost, let us *not* take the way of church history.

Let me give you a real tough test and see if you can pass it. Let's imagine that you have a dear friend, a Christian. Let's also imagine that something comes between the two of you. He does something towards you that is very un-Christian. He does something that a lost man would not even do. In fact, it's the worst thing you ever heard of. Then you discover he's *not* going to stop. He means to make a career out of you. Suddenly you are in a first class crisis. A giant flood is coming upon you. Wave after wave breaks upon your head. The situation is so bad, and so unfair, that you know that you would be justified in whatever you did.

You take it for awhile; you're kind, you're nice. You do all the religious and spiritual things. Then a brand new report comes in.

He's up to even worse. Let me give you some idea of just what he might do. You've been lied about. You've suffered loss. Your friends no longer believe in you. In fact, you're losing friends everywhere. The hour is dark. If you do not speak out, everything is going to be lost. You've been called a liar, a cheat, a heretic, a cultist, a servant of Satan, a false prophet and a Judas. All this by a man who once called you friend. And everyone believes everything he says. Your whole life is being ruined. Emotionally you are wrecked. Your family is living under pressure that no one ought to live under. Your reputation is being destroyed, probably forever, and it's being done internationally. Your whole life, ministry, work, everything is being ended for all time. You realize you're the victim of one of the most vicious attacks you ever heard about or read about, anywhere, at any time.

In the midst of all that, take a moment and stop. Get your emotions together. Don't start thinking ill of that man. Don't start listening to the little man inside of you. Instead, for a moment, walk up to the mountain and look through the eyes of Jesus Christ. Go get the heavenly view (the view *no man* in a crisis *ever* dares admit about his opponent). What is *His* viewpoint? It might amaze you. Despite all the verses of Scripture you could quote against this man, you might be surprised at what *the Lord* thinks of him; he who is your worst enemy. From the Lord's viewpoint, during your blackest hour and such unjust treatment, the Lord looks at your vicious enemy and what does *He* see? The Lord sees a man whom *He* loves very much. A man for whom He died. The Lord is not even angry with this brother. In fact, the Lord is being very patient with him. The Lord is loving him, forgiving him. The Lord is caring for him, and meeting his needs! The Lord is ordering his circumstances. And believe it or not, the Lord is even hearing his prayers! The Lord is taking care of all of his children, and his wife, and his loved ones. Jesus Christ is not offended with that brother. You may be, but the Lord is not. The Lord has not called down plagues on that man. The Lord has not decided to damn him to hell. The Lord is still kind. The Lord is still working in that man's life, trying to lead him further and deeper. Your Lord has not even criticized that man for what he has done to you.

These things are true. To believe less is to open your life to being destroyed by circumstances . . . the very circumstances that await *you* out yonder.

If that is what the Lord is doing, then what shall *you* do? At this black moment, everything in your life is being ripped from under you. How shall you respond? Shall you respond with less than Christ? Remember, Christ is all you need. Remember, Christ is all you want. And thus, Christ is all you should get. The Lord has lacked a people who will walk to a mountain and see things from *His* view. Men who will take Christ, know Christ, and give Christ, no matter who is doing what, no matter what the circumstances.

Furthermore, you are probably going to face a crisis just like the one I described. In that hour you may choose to do something very self-sacrificing, and maybe something even very noble. Yet, ask yourself, "Is it less than Christ?" Lift your face towards the highlands. Look above you. Catch a glimpse of your Lord's ways. See a soil where no footprints are found. See heights that have not been trod for nearly two millenniums.

Seize the banner.

Part Two

CHAPTER 6

Our Relationship to Others

"... dangers from ... my countrymen, dangers from the gentiles ... dangers among false brethren...."   II Cor. 11:26

Paul lived one of the most adventurous, dangerous lives ever lived by mortal man. It was because of his ministry to the Lord's people that he faced almost every situation we will ever encounter. Among those dangers he lists "the Jews" and "the gentiles"— at one time or another both sought his life! We will also face "the Jews" and "the gentiles" even though it be two millenniums later. The situation has changed though. There are no Jewish envoys from Jerusalem, or from the Synagogues, to threaten us. There is no gentile Roman Empire for us to contend with. Yet, in principle, these two elements still exist in the world. They always have, and, until the Lord comes, they always will. Let's look at Paul's "Jews" and his "gentiles." Then we will have some idea of who our modern day counterpart of "the Jews" and "the gentiles" will be. Paul's situation we will not face. But the *equivalent* of his situation we will *undoubtedly* face. And when we do, let us fulfill our mission.

"The gentile," for Paul, was the Roman Empire; but more specifically, the local city governments that opposed him. *"The Jews"* he speaks of were *not*, of course, the entire Jewish race! Paul was himself a Jew! So were over ninety percent of the Christians at the time he wrote these lines! No, by "the Jews" he rather was referring to the men who were the *leaders* of the Jewish

religion. He meant the leaders of the *religious system* of his day, if you please. *"False brethren"* were Christians who were also Jews (or better: Jews who were *also* believers), but who hated Paul because Paul was upsetting Jewish tradition.

All three groups, at one time or another, almost cost Paul his life.

There is one more group to add to this list. We are surrounded by millions of them, yet Paul never so much as met one of them. Of whom do I speak? Of devout Christians in religious organizations. We must figure out how to relate to Christians who are in religious organizations and have no idea of what church life is all about. Paul never met such a creature. There were no religious organizations in his day . . . not with the word "Christian" on them.

CHAPTER 7

The First Peril: The Religious System

Let's look at the record and see what Paul meant by "dangers from the Jews." Who were "the Jews"? What dangers did they put Paul into? Well, just the statistics *alone* are overwhelming. Paul suffered so much at the hands of the Jews . . . that is, the religious system of *his* day.

What the Religious System Did to Paul

Let's outline Paul's life according to the crises he faced which were caused by Jewish religious leaders. It's quite a list.

1. The Early Years.
(1) Immediately after Paul was converted, he tried to preach to the Jews in the synagogue in Damascus. The Jews violently opposed him, his conversion and his message. That was almost certainly his first experience of receiving the thirty-nine lashes. If so, then that was some "coming out party" for a brand new Christian to go through.

(2) On his return to Damascus some years later, the Jews teamed up with the local government (the gentiles) to try to eliminate Paul. He was sneaked out of the city in a basket.

(3) He fled to Jerusalem. There, after only two weeks, he had to flee again. A plot by the Jews was hatched to assassinate him.

2. The First Journey.

On Paul's *first journey*, he raised up four churches. The Jews opposed him in *three* cities:

(1) *Antioch-Pisidia.* The Jews aroused the leading men and women of the city, who in turn drove Paul out of that city.

(2) *Iconium*. The Jews teamed with the gentiles and tried to stone Paul.

(3) *Lystra*. Jews came all the way from Iconium and Antioch for the single purpose of arousing the local citizens against Paul. The result: Paul was stoned, almost fatally.

3. The Second Journey.

During Paul's *second journey*, four more churches were raised up. Once again the Jews opposed him in three cities:

(1) *Thessalonica*. The Jews set the city in an uproar, turned the city government against Paul, and had him officially banished from the city.

(2) *Berea*. The Jews followed Paul from Thessalonica to Berea, stirred up crowds against him, and once more forced him to flee.

(3) *Corinth*. Twice Paul faced the Jews: at the outset of his visit; and eighteen months later when they rose up the second time, as one man, to rid the city of him.

4. The Third Journey.

On his *third journey*, Paul visited only one new city. We'll hold off for just a moment to see what it was that the Jews did to Paul on this journey. The reason I'd like to wait a moment is because it was there in the city of Ephesus that Paul scaled new heights . . . new heights for the banner! He raised the highest standard possible in his attitude toward those who opposed him.

You have just read the list of what Paul went through at the hands of the Jews from the time he was converted until the end of his third voyage. Quite a record.[1]

---

[1]*Add to this list the five beatings he received from the Jews. They are not listed because we do not know when or where they took place.*

Now we are prepared to ask the question, what was Paul's attitude toward these men? What was Paul's attitude toward a religious system that treated him so horribly?

The Story of Ephesus

Let's return to the close of Paul's third journey. He is in Ephesus. He is about to leave to visit Corinth. From there, he hopes to go to Jerusalem. At least he is going to try. But right now he can't get out of town. He sits with his back to the wall, his face toward the door. There are men in the area, devout Jews, who would kill him if they had the chance. (We will hear more of these people a little later.)

This new situation—attempted murder—is nothing more than the climax of nearly twenty years of persecution which Paul has endured from the hands of the Jews. Today their effort has turned into an all-out, organized crusade. It appears that Ephesus is fraught with spies, lookouts, signals, plans and plots. It's almost an armed invasion which has hit Asia Minor. All are there for one reason: to murder Paul.

So this is what Paul received from the Jews on his third journey! Add this to the long list we made a few minutes ago. How would you feel? After twenty years of this kind of treatment, what would be *your* attitude toward a religious system that treated you this way? Well, we are going to find out Paul's attitude. Right about now he is going to write a letter. In this letter he tells us his exact attitudes toward these vicious people.

Paul's Attitude Toward the Religious System

"Twenty years, Paul! Stoned by them, beaten by them, lied about, chased, mobbed by them. They have tried to kill you. They have attempted to undermine your reputation, destroy the nine or ten churches you have raised up. Your body is gnarled, ripped, racked with pain and virtually destroyed because of them. Your work on earth would have been far easier, far bigger if these people had just left you alone. *And you have never once spoken a critical word about them.* They have hurt you. If they succeed in killing you, they will then most likely go after the churches. They will attempt to destroy these churches, too, if they possibly can.''

This is the scene as Paul attempts to round out his third journey; and with *this* scene as the backdrop, I would like you to watch what happens next. Paul manages to sneak out of Ephesus and ultimately reach Corinth. While in Corinth, Paul decides to write a letter to a little band of believers in another faraway city . . . a city he has never seen, a group of Christians he has never visited. He wants to write a clear letter, a thorough letter, a letter that deals with all the issues they will face—for they are only just now getting started—and Paul knows he may never live long enough to go visit them. They need all the advice, help, and certainly *warnings,* that he can give. They are so few, the situation in their faraway city so fragile. They could be snuffed out at any time. The least bit of trouble would probably destroy them. This letter will *have* to take the place of a visit.

The city? Rome! He hopes to go there someday (journey number four), but chances are a lot better that he will be dead in a few days!

Since this letter must take the place of a visit, one thing for sure must be dealt with, Paul. Warn them about the Jews! Tell them what they have done to you for nearly two decades. Prepare them, Paul! Those people, who right now are trying to kill you, even as you take up quill and ink . . . blister them, Paul! At least *warn* those Christians in Rome. This may be your last chance (nay, your *only* chance) to deal with this subject. Prepare the Roman Christians for the inevitable day when the Jews will come there too, to rise up against them.

Sure enough, Paul did pick up his pen, and sure enough, he

did talk about the Jews. With his back pressed to the wall, with one eye on the door, with the knowledge he could be stabbed to death at any second, a body wrecked and racked with what the Jews had done to it, with twenty years of such hair-raising, blood-freezing confrontations burned in his memory, Paul writes . . . and he writes about the *Jews*. About the men in the religious system.

In fact, he wrote around three pages about the Jews. He probably wrote those three pages with his door locked. Go read them! As you do, remember that this was penned by a man who could have been killed at any moment, a man who had suffered unparalleled abuse for well over fifteen years. Read those pages carefully. Try to find *one word* of animosity, one word of bitterness, just one negative word of any kind! Paul doesn't even refer to the things they had done to him or said about him! There is no rebuttal to their attacks and lies. There is no defense. Most incredibly, there is *no* warning! There is not one word, not one hint of the crisis he is presently in.

Paul writes this letter as though he never had a problem in his life with those people. Try to find any bitterness or criticism. There is none. What is there, then? Look closely. If you do, you will notice one of the most glorious statements in all Holy Writ.

In all divinely inspired writings, there are found only three men who have made the statement that they were willing to take someone else's place in hell . . . in hell, if you please . . . in order to see those people saved. Moses was the first man to ever make such an extreme statement. Of course, the second man was the Lord Jesus Christ. (In fact, He did die for us.) The third man? Brother Paul! And where did he make this statement? And of whom did he make it? He made it in the book of Romans, in one of the darkest hours of his life, when the very people he was writing about (the people he was willing to be accursed for, so that they might be saved) were seeking to kill him!

Can you see, then, how he viewed this whole crisis he was in? He wasn't mad or resentful. He was heartbroken, for *their* sakes.

Paul, who had spent his life being ripped to pieces, pressed out of measure . . . this man Paul, who had lava-hot hatred poured on him every day of his life, who had on endless occasions seen the progress of the kingdom come to a complete stop . . . this man—who had faced death at the hands of his fellow countrymen, the Jews, so many times—pens these incredible words:

"I say the truth in Christ, I lie not, my conscience also bearing me witness in the Holy Ghost, that I have great heaviness and continual sorrow in my heart. For I could wish that myself were accursed from Christ for my brethren . . . . " Romans 9:1-3

Paul spoke for people who had dealt him nearly two decades of unparalleled misery. His was a prayer that was absolutely incredible.

And now, my dear brothers, I believe you understand what I am talking about; for it was there, in *that* high place, thrust into the earth by Paul, that the banner was last seen waving. Yes, *a man* has actually carried the standard *that* high!!! What a standard!

You and I need to be conscious of all this. As a group of people, we need to know where the standard was, and we need to recognize the possible abuses we face in the future . . . at the hands of the religious system . . . and what our conduct must be.

It does not matter who they are: Jew, Greek, Moslem, Buddhist or Christian. No matter what they *say* against you, no matter what they *do* to you, no matter how great a price they force you to pay, how difficult they make the task for you, nor how total the destruction you must witness around you . . . you must remember Paul's attitude toward the religious system of his day: "I have great heaviness and continued sorrow. I would that *I* might be accursed."

Brothers! Sisters! Now you know what your calling is. We are called to forbear with other men who do these kinds of things, and to forbear as well as Paul did; to forbear *that* long, *that* much, toward *all* men.

This is where the banner was planted nearly two thousand years ago; planted there by a man named Paul. There needs to be a people living on this earth who will take that banner back up those slopes and plant it in that same high place . . . for *this* is our mission.

CHAPTER 8

A Closer Look at the Religious System

We have seen something of Paul's incredible attitude toward the religious system of his day. Now we must look at the religious system of our day and figure out our relationship to it.

Why do this? Because Paul spoke of "perils" from this vicinity! You see, we may not venture far afield, or we may go to the ends of the earth. But of *this* you can be sure: In every city to which we may journey, no matter what country or what continent, whether near or far, there you will face a religious system. There is *some* kind of a religious system to be faced in every city on earth. We are bound to bump into it.

In Nepal, it may be the religious system formulated by Buddhists; in Afghanistan, one constructed by Moslems; in Rome, a religious system built by Catholics; in East Texas, one built by Baptists; and in Isla Vista, one erected by inter-denominational organizations. Go to the next town or the next continent, but be sure, if religion is there, a system is there.

And if *future* church history can be judged by *past* church history, then you can be certain of this: At some point that system will rise up against you. So, at least, has it been in all ages past.

You have just heard me say that the religious system will one day oppose you, no matter where you go. You have perhaps also heard me say, "Have nothing to do with the religious system." Now, those are both strong words. I had better have a mighty good reason for such statements, mighty good indeed. I do. You will see why when you see what the religious system really is.

First, there is a big difference in saying, "Have nothing to do with the religious system," and saying, "Have nothing to do with other Christians." If we ever say, "Have nothing to do with other Christians," we are in big trouble. If we talk like that or act like that, we will be sectarian and exclusive. We must be totally open to all Christians. More open than anyone else on earth. Christ died for all of us. There simply must be no test of fellowship between any believers. None! (Well, maybe there is one: Out-and-out, open, rank, unrepented-of immorality.) Open to all believers, everywhere. No barriers. The door open, the hinges off.

But the religious system? That is a different matter, If we get involved in the religious system again, we are in *big* trouble. Why? The reasons are formidable and they are endless. We *will* look at some of the reasons. We should have nothing to do with the religious system! Why? The answer is a mind-blower. Let's look.

We will begin by tracing the origin of the religious system throughout history, right on down to our age. In so doing, we can clearly see *what* the religious system is in principle as well as *who* makes up that system in our age.

I use the term religious system. What do I mean by this term? I would like to clearly tell you what I mean when I speak of the religious system. The best way to do this is to trace (1) the origin of systematization and (2) the origin of religion. Perhaps a clear definition will then emerge.

The History of System

The words "systematization" and "organization" are words very similar in meaning. I could say "organized religion" as well as I could "the religious system." What is the origin of "system" and "organization"? Well, the answer is a shocker!

God is the author of organization. In fact, the whole organizational pattern of western civilization—that system of structure that pervades and permeates every facet of our daily lives . . . be it medicine, education, politics, business, labor, civic activity, social work, or whatever — was invented by God.

Wow! God invented organization?! Then why am I so dead set against it in church life? The reason is simple. Organization may control the entire activity of all mankind, *and* God may have invented the thing . . . *but* . . . and that is a very big *but* . . . organization was never meant for *man!* Man was never to have anything to do with organization or systematization. For man to succumb to structuralization is to place on himself the ways of an alien life form. Put it another way: For man to allow himself to become part of a systematized order is to *enslave* himself to the lifestyle of alien beings from another universe. Or to put it a little less dramatically, God invented organization for angels and not for man. *Angels,* if you please, turned around and super-imposed their civilization — their systematization, their angelic organizational life, their culture — on *man*. Angels have imposed their own innate way of functioning on that creature who was intended to be the freest creature in the universe! Man! Man has no business submitting to angelic ways. Their civilization and their systematization is organic to them, but alien to us. Man was created for absolute freedom. A group of angels are using their innate bend toward organization to enslave man. By enslaving man they thwart God's primary purpose from creation. Sounds like something right out of Star Trek, doesn't it? Aliens from another universe seeking to enslave man.

Now that, dear brother, will give you some basis for understanding why I am so utterly opposed to system and organization in the Christian faith, especially in church life!

The Spiritual History of Organization

I would like to re-tell the story of the origin of organization. We will use the record of spiritual history to do so. After looking at the origin and history of systematization in *spiritual* history, I would like to then go over to secular history and see what it tells us. You will find the two interlock.

On the first day of creation, God created the Heavenlies. When He did, He also created heavenly beings to populate this heavenly realm. Now what was God's purpose in creating these beings? They were formed for a two-fold purpose: to be His servants and to become the servants of man. As to gender, He created angelic beings neuter. They are not men. They are not women. They do not breed nor procreate. There are exactly as many angels today as on the first day of creation; no more . . . no less. They have a created life in them that goes on forever. God created angels as wondrous beings, and as a numberless army. In fact, they are set up as legions. (The New Testament seems to imply that the organizational set-up of heaven and the organizational set-up of the Roman Empire's army were *identical!* Now whom do you figure copied whom?)

Heaven had the following structure: God. Free. Without law. No restrictions. Above even liberty. As Creator He is by nature King, Lord, Ruler and Potentate. Beneath are the angels. He divided this angelic host into three equally numbered divisions. Over each of these three divisions He set a glorious archangel. Take a look at that. What do you see? God had set up the original *chain-of-command!* This is a system of "order from the top" that permeates down to the lower levels. This is a structure pattern familiar to anyone who has ever been in the military. Remember, though, the idea and the practice did not begin with some ancient army. No. It began in the Heavenlies. The "pyramid" structure of organization. The "flow chart," the "pecking order," the "chain-of-command" are all terms we hear used to describe this set-up.

Now comes the sad part of this story. One of those three archangels led a revolt in the Heavenlies. For this insurrection he was cast out of the heavens to the earth. With him went his legions. One-third of all angels were cast out of the heavenlies. They would have to find a new home somewhere else in the universe. Lucifer came to the regions around earth. He led the fallen angels with him. They came according to inherent order. Behold, organization

84

got to earth by *treason.* Organization was never intended for planet earth. It is an alien thing. It is foreign to earth and to man. What, then, was to be man's social pattern? Man, like the God in whose image he was created, was not designed to be systematized, organized, or controlled. Man, like God, was made for total freedom. Man was not ordained to be controlled or ruled. *Man*—like God—was to *rule!*

Now the plot thickens. Can you see the situation? With the coming of Lucifer, man and fallen angels shared the same territory. Lucifer, archangel over one-third of the heavenly host, now gives his full attention to deceiving man. He succeeds in causing man to fall. Man is introduced to sin. Just as God had once banished Lucifer from his abode in the Heavenlies, God now must banish man from the garden. Fallen man is turned out of the garden to find himself a place to live outside the garden. He must live, a fallen man on a fallen planet.

At this point man was outside God's presence. He was also naked, and feeling every inch of it. He sensed his need for protection. Specifically, Cain built a city called Enoch. This place of protection became a wicked thing, and other cities like it soon grew up in other parts of earth. God destroyed these places of protection by means of a flood. Nonetheless, soon after the flood, man was back doing the same old things.

That brings us to the birth of the city of Babel. It appears that it is here that Satan first succeeds—embryonically—in superimposing his angelic organization on human activity. A very fallen man named Nimrod founded Babel. Or did he? Wasn't the true founder one from the skies? From Babel on Satan gradually, but thoroughly, drew man into a systematized manner of life. In our day, man actually likes systematization of human activity, even brags about it and often gloats in it. He will unhesitantly persecute, imprison and kill anyone who in any way threatens this "system" of living.

Up until Babel we have been telling spiritual history as recorded in Scripture. This is history that is God-authored. I think it is very interesting that at this specific point secular history takes over and traces the development of this very same subject.

The Story of Organization in Secular History

Secular history tells us of the successive rise of four great, ancient Kingdoms: Egypt (about 1400 B.C.); Assyria (about 700 B.C.); Babylon (550 B.C.); and Persia (500 B.C.).

Assyria was the granddaddy of human systematization. They were the first world-wide conquerors. They were military people and imposed their military organizational pattern on every country, city and person they captured. Babylon—a revived Babel—in turn conquered the Assyrians.

Now Babylon was also a military dictatorship, so every facet of human life was set up like the army itself . . . chain-of-command. This was man in angelic order! It was at this time the pattern was set. Soon, every man in every "civilized" country on earth would be raised in this pattern. You can almost say it is in our blood. For sure it is unmoveably embedded in every circuit of our thought pattern. Satan's trap sprung. Man was part of a system so all-pervading that every area of his life was a system, each system set in a yet greater system.

Yes, on the day the trap sprang, every man could look up and say he reported to someone above him. At the top of the chain was Nebuchadnezzar. Or was he? Actually, one of the ancient Hebrew prophets said that *Lucifer* was head.

And today. Look at any organizational chart of *anything*. Everyone reports to someone above. Who is at the top?

Darius I

Now Babylon was soon overthrown and conquered by Persia. Very shortly there arose one of the greatest, most titanic figures of human history, a man who has influenced everyone of our lives . . . Darius the Great (521-486 B.C.).

This man conquered nation after nation. He set up a monolithic rule that stretched from India to Greece, one of the largest empires of all time. He did all this in about 500 B.C. How? Let a historian tell you.

86

The Persians made two outstanding contributions to the ancient world:
The organization of their empire and their religion. Both of these
contributions have had considerable influence on our western world.
The system of imperial administration was inherited by Alexander the
Great, adopted by the Roman Empire, and eventually bequeathed to
modern Europe. [1]

Interesting isn't it? Now you know how your government got its structure; your school, your university, the medical profession, politics,
automobile manufacturers, retail stores, the police, the army, the company you work for, the civilization you live in.

Darius I gave it to you. Don't forget that!

But what has that got to do with us staying out of the religious
system? Plenty! The religious system you and I have inherited came to
us — not from the Lord of the New Testament — but by one of the
greatest military geniuses of all time. From Darius, one of the greatest
organizers known to history. He is one of the greatest names in history. But he got his ideas from the land he conquered: Babylon. Who
was this Darius? Who is this man that all western political and religious organizations of all the ages have copied?

Well, the fellow was a Zoroastrian. He was one of the cruelest
monsters ever to pour blood on the pages of history. Furthermore, his
greatest imitator was Rome. Hold on to your hat. His second greatest
imitator was the church!

You doubt a little, maybe?

Then I call secular history to the witness stand once more. D.C.
Trueman tells us in *The Pageant of the Past* some of the contributions
of the Roman Empire. (Please recall that this empire — this military
machine — took its pattern from Darius, who got it from Babylon.)

Finally, from the Romans came a magnificent organization: the Empire.
The church modeled its administration units [!] on Roman political sub-
divisions, and in time the successors of St. Peter, the bishop of Rome,
came to exercise a certain authority so that the church, like the Empire.

---

[1] Trueman, *The Pageant of the Past*, pg. 105.

had its chain of command *and carefully linked administrations. No other religion could boast such a complete and efficient organization.*[2]

I hardly see how it could be stated more clearly. Here we are told that the Catholic Church was patterned after the Roman Empire and was, in fact, the best organized religion going. Some student, the Catholic Church. But it has had some good imitators, too. Who? The structure of all great denominations today are exact replicas of the organizational structure of the Catholic Church, of the Roman Empire—of Greece, Persia, Babylon, and angels! If you wish to be part of that, wade in. Please forgive me if I pass up such a golden opportunity. I prefer to spend an exciting evening in the laundry room watching my clothes tumble dry. No, I do not intend to be part of the religious system.

Now let's tie the two stories together; spiritual history and secular history.

The Story: Spiritual and Secular

God created organization when He created the angels. He aligned them in an intricate hierarchical pattern. This chain-of-command exists even today among *all* angels.

Long ago, when Lucifer was cast out of the heavenlies and was forced to make his home here in the visible realm, he took one-third of the angels with him. He ran his legions by chain-of-command. Lucifer had a scheme. He designed to ensnare man, to distract man from God, to break man's dependence on God. To do this, he introduced man to something called "civilization." He did it little by little at first. What is this thing called *civilization?* It is nothing but angelic order. Satan got man acquainted with *his* ways. Gradually he wove man right into the order *he* presided over. By Satan's scheme both angels and men were now interwoven into one civilization, one system, one ruler. Satan began in

---

2 Ibid., pg. 311.

cities. Civilization is enlarged "city life." City life was enlarged, duplicated in jumbo size, to take in principalities, then regions, then nations, then continents, and finally the entire world. This was joined—interlocked—into the order of his angels.

Scripture tells us that Nimrod was the founder of civilization. He seems to have been the man who introduced the systematized angelic order to fallen man. It was Nimrod who founded Babel.

History picks up the story here. In a later era Babel was renewed. New Babylon—as history often calls it—saw its organizational pattern picked up by the Medes and Persians. They gave it to the whole planet. Later the Greeks appropriated it from the Medes. Greece organized just about every facet of its life in this manner.

Rome conquered Greece. You need to know that Rome gave our modern world its whole present organizational pattern. That pattern so utterly, totally, pervades the earth, cutting across all cultures, philosophies and politics that we have a hard time even trying to imagine life by any other pattern. *Everything* we touch today in human activity is organized just like ancient Rome!

Now Scripture refers to this whole intricate web as "the world system." Satan systematized man into a complex lifestyle. He totally succeeded in distracting man from God. What we call civilization is in fact only angelic order imposed on man. One system. No more. Just one. That system is now imposed on *every* human movement. Look about you and see every unit of social contact arranged in this identical pattern.

It's like little gears inside bigger gears, inside one big wheel, or small mosaic patterns inside large ones, making up—finally— one vast mosaic. Let me illustrate.

The entire world of education is but one piece of that vast mosaic. Inside the world of education are little miniatures of the big one. School boards, schools, universities; then going up the chain is the state educational organization and the federal education structure. Step back. Look. You grasp the sight of one vast educational system. But, this thing called the educational system is only one of many areas of life. The world of education is but one of the gears, one of the mosaics. Medicine is another, business yet another, industry yet one more. Step back farther. Now what do you see? You see them all combined into one great worldwide system. This system fits snugly right into angelic order.

All right, holding this much of history before us, I think we are ready to continue.

The Church: Enter Anti-establishmentarianism

Along came the Church! The year is 30 A.D. The place is Jerusalem, Israel. Rome is the occupying force of both Jerusalem and Israel. Everything in sight is systematized. And now, lo and behold, the Church steps into history. This beautiful, young girl is the one exception to this whole, long story. The church was, and is, anti-world system. The church is *not* an organization. The church is anti-establishment. She does not operate by chain-of-command. The church is the one thing Lucifer doesn't head. Jesus Christ is *direct* Head of His Church, His Body. No organization is she, but a Woman! She is not kin to a wristwatch. She is alive. A woman. The fiancee of Jesus Christ!

(By the way, the church has suffered from only one enemy in all her history: the world system. There is one particular system inside the world system that persecutes the church the most. Obviously, that is the *religious* system. Yes, the political segment of the world system has a go at it from time to time, too. But the religious system has the highest score.)

Well, the church did very well for the first 200 years. She, like the angels, had a life style that came from God. But her life system was not chain-of-command. The church was not patterned after the organizational pattern of angels. She has order, yes, but she is *not* organized. Then how is she organizationally constituted? She is *not* organizationally constituted. She is a living creature. Only "things" are organizations. She is not a thing, she is a human being . . . a woman. Perhaps you can't grasp the idea of the church without organizational structure. There are several reasons for that. None good.

The first is, the word "church" has been associated in your mind with an organization that calls itself the church. Well, it isn't. Even if it calls itself the church it is still just an organization. A *religious* organization. Secondly, *you've* got an organizational pattern soldered right into your head. You can hardly conceptualize anything else.

God's Own Life Style

When God organized angels, He put them in a system. They were a lower life form. Because He was all alone, as far as His *own* life form is concerned, you could not tell whether or not He Himself would be organized if He lived in (beg your pardon) a society of gods. Well, today He is *not* alone. He has children, and a family, and a house. We are that house and that family. He is Father. He is Head. But He is Head of each of us individually. Get that. That is totally opposite to chain-of-command. Look at your own family. It is not organized. Every person reports to the head. Your family is a living entity. (We will not deal with the subject of the organic order of the church, but only pause to say, *emphatically*, that the early church was never put into a structured pattern, not by God, not by angels, not by men.)

Point: When God was alone no one could know for certain if he would live, like angels, in a tight structure. He got His own race beginning with Jesus Christ! Then the matter was settled. No! The family of God is not structured!

The Church Falls Victim to Organization

By the year 200 A.D., unfortunately, the church was slipping. Again and again persecution had taken the best of her people. But the greater villain was not persecution, but *time* itself. The environment was gradually winning out. The ways of the world system were creeping into the churches of both Italy and Asia Minor. (The North African churches fared quite a bit better.)

To understand what really took place at this crucial, tragic period in the life of the church, we need to also see what was happening to the Empire itself. Three times in its long history, the Roman Empire peaked in organizational glory. The first high ascent into organizational greatness was the period of Julius and Augustus Caesar. Previous to that, a set of checks and balances had prevented a super-colossal structure. Later, Hadrian refurbished and refined the Empire's vast chain-of-command. Finally, Constantine was to perfect it. Perhaps not since Darius I had organization been so perfected. It is incredible that it was in this period — the finest hour of organizational glory — that the early church was so completely swept into the world system.

Weep.

Here is the story. In the early 300's Constantine had some kind of conversion to Christ. (The quality of that conversion is one of the most speculated-about events in history.) In fact, Constantine must be listed as the first medieval Christian: 90 percent Christian in name; 90 percent pagan in thought. Because of his conversion and his ascension to the throne, by 313 Constantine was able to lift the pressure of persecution off the much-decimated churches.

Until that hour, Constantine, like all Emperors before him, was not only head of the Empire, but head of every department in the Empire. (By the way, he could only *think* in those terms. He was head of *everything.*) That meant he was the highest priest, the pontiff maximus in paganism. Well, he *began* to draw the early church into his organization. As a result, over the next 75 Years. (1) Christianity became one of the official religions of the Empire, right beside paganism. This meant direct grants of tax money to the church. It also meant that the church was now but one department in the government of the Empire. (2) Gradually paganism was squeezed completely out, tax support ended, its property was given to Christianity, and all religious tax support went to the church. As these events evolved the church gradually took on the organizational structure of all other departments in the Roman system. The beautiful girl succumbed; a tight-knit religious organization emerged to replace her. The early church vanished. Only her name remained. The name "church" was pasted on a religious organization.

Words such as "deacon" and "elder" remained. (Some new words came along—new to Christians—such as "cardinal" and "clergy" . . . both taken right out of paganism.) But though some labels remained, the newly imposed structure was purely Babylonian. Look at the structure of the Catholic Church as it eventually emerged. At the bottom were priests, then bishops, then archbishops, then cardinals—with the Emperor at the top of the pyramid. Oops, the Emperor was *one removed* from the top.

This state of affairs continued for several hundred years. Eventually, the Empire collapsed. When it did, many small nations emerged from the ruin. Instead of one Empire—one nation—there were now many small nations. Now every one of those nations had an organizational set-up. I need not tell you how each nation was organized. You know. Each nation was an organizational miniature of the old Roman Empire. In each case— without exception—Roman Catholicism was the one and only official religion of every nation. Previously, Catholicism had been the one and only religion of an Empire. Now it was the one and only religion of each of the nations formed out of the collapsed Empire. Once the official religion of the Empire, it now became an *inter*-national religion. Furthermore, the structure of Catholicism was still the same as it was back in the 300's . . . chain-of-command.

All of this is the record of a terrible, tragic rape of what had once been. During all this period—from about 325 onward—a few Christians refused to belong to this gigantic religious organization. For that refusal they were persecuted . . . and killed. These people—this other group of Christians in church history—discovered, as did Paul (and as will we) what it meant to taste the displeasure of the religious system.

The religious system—an organization—is the natural enemy of the church, an organic being.

The Place of Organization During the Reformation

Well, at last the situation changed. Along came 1517 and Martin Luther. Luther lived in a country called Saxony. This country had as its official state religion, of course, the Catholic Church. Luther broke with the Roman Catholic Church. And so did Saxony. This was unprecedented! For the first time in 1500 years there was a nation in Europe that did *not* have Catholicism as its official religion.

Saxony threw Catholicism out of the department of religion. In its place there was designated a brand new group . . . the Lutherans. Every nation in Christendom had Catholicism as its official religion—except Saxony!!! Revolutionary!

Well, the Lutherans came in with a new theology. Their teachings were radically different. In came new rituals, new words, new freedom, and new titles for their leaders. ("Priest" gave way to "pastor.")

It all looked great. But Luther did something unwittingly. He kept the same organizational pattern!

In a way, he had no choice. Here is why.

Saxony was organized exactly like the Roman Empire had been, long ago. Saxony was a miniature of the ancient Empire. Of course, all lesser organizations in Saxony were structured after the pattern of the King's government. So when Lutheranism was inserted as the new, official religion . . . the labels changed, yes, but the pattern of organization remained virtually identical to that of the Roman Catholic Church. Structurally, Lutheranism fit into the Saxony way of life in the same way all the rest of Saxony's society did . . . by chain-of-command. Amazing.

Well, the story goes that soon other nations began to break with Catholicism. Next Scandinavia took Lutheranism as its new state religion. England, under Henry VIII got a new church.

Scotland yet another. Theologies were different. Names were different. Rituals were different. But the "chain-of-command" concept remained unchanged.

By now the course was set. Each nation had *one* official religion. The religion might differ from nation to nation, *but the structural pattern was always the same.* (In every one of these nations the Christians who would not align themselves with this structure ... were persecuted.)

Organization After the Reformation

Now let us observe the next new development. A little later on the Baptist, Congregationalist, Covenant (and even later the Pentecostal) denominations emerged. These groups were a little different. Dissenters! They were never an official state religion in *any* country. No state taxes ever went into their offering plates to keep them afloat. These are what Europeans call "Free Evangelicals": free of state control and state support. Their labels were different, their theology radically different, their ritual (yes, they have it) much simpler. But the organizational set-up in each is as old as Rome; no, as old as Babylon. Nay! As old as the angels!

(Some groups appoint their leaders, some choose by committee, some are democratic and do it by vote . . . and each denomination used an entirely different set of names. But in all of them, the "flow chart" *is* "chain-of-command."

When I was a young minister, for a short time I was invited to work closely with the world's largest charismatic denomination. In the process, I received a tour of their whole headquarters. I recall being told that they had studied all the other major denominations to see which had the best, most dynamic, most effective organizational set-up. They discovered (as you might guess) that America's *largest* Protestant denomination was the most streamlined and best organized. Consequently, they told me proudly, they had copied the organizational set-up of the denomination I was raised in . . . copied it from top to bottom. It was a thing to boast about and be proud of. My point? The concept of organizing our religion is in our veins, even the marrow of our bones.

The Present Day State of Organization

Well, since the dissenters, major denominations have pretty well stopped being born. In the place of the birth of new denominations, there has more recently arisen the "non-profit, non-denominational religious organization." Now these folks come right out and say it: "We are an organization!" And they are, too!

In the 1700's and 1800's when a strong, religious man wanted to do something, he probably went out and started a new denomination. That is passe now. (Besides, today just about all the theological disputes have already been chewed over.) Today, such a man gets a tax-exempt status and founds a religious organization. Instead of pastor, churches, and denominational headquarters, there are "staff," "centers," and . . . ah-hum . . . just "headquarters." Essentially, at least in structure, there is little difference in the flow chart of a denomination and the flow chart of a non-profit religious organization.

I have often visited the headquarters of the world's largest such organization. They boast of their organizational efficiency. I was once told (I do not know if the story is true, but the point is nonetheless obvious) that a graduate student of the Harvard School of Business studied their organization carefully and concluded that it was as well-organized and as efficient as General Motors!

Yes, all religious organizations and all denominations are virtually the same in structure: The structure of Nimrod, Darius, Alexander the Great, Julius Ceasar, Constantine, King George, Washington, Jefferson, Napolean, Hitler, Churchill, and Henry Ford. My dear brother, denominations and tax exempt religious movements are all organizations. That is *all* they are . . . no more. *Religious* organizations. Those things are *not* the Bride of Christ.

I do not know, dear reader, how you feel after reading all this.

Personally, I burn to be through with such practices and from such distant meanderings from the Lord's intent. Church history is perhaps the most tragic story of tongue or pen . . . as we think of what might have been if Christian men would have never adopted, or would now abandon, organizational structure. And that point underscores *our mission.* We will catch it from the religious institutions—if the future can be judged by the past—for not being organized. (Strangely, though organized Christendom covers the earth, yet this vast organization seems to be terribly threatened when it sees rising around it a people who don't become organized. It panics at seeing *any* Christians outside of structure. History says the religious leaders will do *anything* to stop such a move.)

Few things demand restoring more than the simple matter of Christians gathering as the body of Christ, outside of predictable organizational pattern. Our course is clear. We will not be part of institutionalization. Can you not see that God's Kingdom—given to man—must remain outside angelic order?

The "Religious" Part of the System

I have traced the system; it originated in the heavenlies! But I have also used the term "religous *system*" and "*organized* religion." Perhaps, before we go any further, we had better give a little attention to the first word in that phrase. What do I mean by a "*religious*" system?

If I were to state that Buddhism is a system, or Hinduism is a system, you would agree. Each is a religious system. But what of Judaism? Is it? Yes. Was it always? No. At one time it was the very work of God on the earth. During the days of Moses and the days of David, the living God was having His way in a group of people. But one day God departed from Judaism. Nonetheless, Judaism continued . . . without God. Behold, a religious movement! Here was a religious unit void of the very God that brought it into being. Yet, it survives even until this hour. But how does it survive? Well, by many means, but one means it uses to survive (and that is absolutely necessary for survival when God isn't with you) is to get organized. This is what Judaism did. In fact, Judaism had *already* done this *long* before Paul came along.

I guess men in every age who are outside religious systematization are destined to clash with somebody's religious system that exists in his particular age. The one Paul came up against was Judaism. (The Anabaptists came up against the Catholics. Nee, Bakht Singh, and Prem Pradhan came up against the good guys: evangelical Christians . . . who proved to be able to persecute with the best of them.) Chances are, Judaism will *not* be the religious system you will bump into out there. But be sure, one *is* out there. "Danger from the Jews" is a fact of life to Christians outside organized religion. Some religious system is out there waiting.

Judaism was once God's work. God left it and it got organized. (Or was it the other way around?) Later, Judaism became the very enemy of God's new work on the earth. That which began as the work of God became the enemy of God. If you can find no other reason to fear getting organized, fear for *this* reason alone.

Buddhism is a religious system. Judaism is a religious system. But can this also happen to the Christian faith? Can a Christian work that is of God later become the very enemy of a new work of God?

Did this tragedy eventually befall even the early church? Did it, with the passing centuries, get organized and become the very enemy of God, or is God still with the early church today? Is it possible God left even the early church and moved on to another people?

I know what you are thinking: "The early church doesn't exist any more; it ended in about 300 A.D. How can you ask, 'Is He still with the early church *today*?' " Don't be too sure. The early church might not have ended . . . as we are often told. Perhaps it does still exist . . . today!

When I was a young man in seminary, I learned two teachings on "What Happened to the Early Church?" Some said the early church is no more. Others taught the early church survived as little hidden groups in the Alps, Spain, etc. Well, I have studied church history since I was seventeen years old, and here are the facts as I have discovered them. Neither of the two statements above has much historical validity. The major evidence, as much as we hate to admit it, lies somewhere else.

The early church still exists, *in an unbroken line!* It does not exist in its original state, to be sure. But it is here; in a long, evolved, corrupted, radically changed, but nonetheless *unbroken* lineage. Today, the early church is called the Roman Catholic Church! The early church is here, plus Constantine, plus a lethal dose of paganism, plus organization, plus 1700 years of traditions, plus who knows what else.

In about 325 A.D. the early church married Roman paganism. It was an unholy marriage; something pagan, something sacred. God walked out during the ceremony. Since that time the early church has become a religious organization. And God? He went somewhere else to do *His work* with another people. (God is not sectarian.)

Sorry if that shakes you up. God will start brand new tomorrow if He finds it necessary to do so. He will drop one people and adopt another at any time! He will carry on *His* work. So, you see, Buddhism *was, is* and always *has* been a religious organization; Judaism *became* a religious system; and the early church also *became* a systematized religion.

What of present-day evangelical Christianity? Ah, ha. Now we get a little uncomfortable. Christianity today *is* about 99 percent organization and one percent church life. (That's being gracious.) All of us who are born-again believers grew up in nothing more than a religious organization. Repeat, an organization—religious in purpose. That is Christianity! That is where the believers are.

What is Christendom today? It is a patch quilt of a lot of movements which, somewhere back there, God was more or less blessing. But long ago He took His blessing away. (Some of them He was *never* with.) Today they are but organizations, religious in nature. A good-sized hunk of Christianity is simply the remains of something God has departed from. Where has He gone? He has gone to call out a people, like Abraham, to give their lives to Jesus Christ and to know Him supremely, to know Him only.

What Is the Religious System In Your Lifetime?

It is time we came to grips with this question: Just what is the religious system today? After that we shall consider what is to be our relationship to it.

Do all the religious organizations of our day—denominations and tax exempt organizations included—belong to the world system? Are they one of the systems within the greater system?

First, there is no question of the Scripture's teaching that there is a world system. But is a denominational church part of that system? Is a religious organization?

I would like to answer that by inviting you to an imaginary little town in East Texas.

Here in our imaginary town you will find the educational system. That little educational system is set up exactly the way Darius the Great set up his empire over 2,000 years ago. In this town is also the business world. Ditto. You will also find a political system in this town. Babylon revisited. On and on we could go: recreation, entertainment, medicine, government. Now put them all together. What do you have? Well, you have something folks there affectionately call "our community," and "our little town." That town is, in fact, made up of many parts, or slices . . . like a giant pie. Put it together and you have commmunity life, or better, "civilization." Many small systems and organizations making up the one great whole: a town in East Texas. Well, right in the middle of that community, right square in the middle of all those other slices—and a *very* intricate part of the pie—is the religious system of that community. Not only is it part and parcel, it is expected, even required, to be part and parcel. I know. I was a pastor in East Texas!

This is very difficult to explain, but the religious system *is* part of the world system. Yes, and we denominational pastors were part of that system. (Yes, and my denomination was, and is, organized . . . to the teeth. That's no criticism, that is a quote. They stated, boasted, advertised and flaunted the fact.)

We pastors visit the sick, bury the dead, bring the invocation at civic, educational, and political gatherings. And, shades of Nero, we even go up to the press box, take the microphone and pray down heavenly blessings on a football massacre that is about to begin. We serve on committees of the Red Feather, United Way, Red Cross, Boy Scouts and other benevolent fund raising ventures. Obviously, we didn't see the mortal conflict going on between the kingdom of this world and the kingdom of God. We did not see, do not see, that the church is also a civilization of sorts; but one distinct and separated from the civilization of man; a kingdom in direct conflict with *that* civilization which East Texas folks call "community life." Yet there we are, a religious organization that is an integral part of the life of "our little community."

But just as bad—if not worse than being an integral part of this system—we are identical to it in structure. A typical Baptist church is an organization. (If you don't believe that, I recommend you go join one. We were so organized we could make a Swiss watch wind up with envy.) Again, that's no criticism of Baptists. They glory in it. I repeat, the church of Jesus Christ is a woman, a living organism, not a thing, not an inorganic organization. Systems belong to angels and—since the fall—to the ways of fallen man. The church belongs to the family of God.

Christendom has, by and large, for the last 1700 years, been part of the world system and it has been structured like all the secular institutions of the earth. Yet, there have *always* been Christians in every age who would not conform to this tradition. Peacefully, quietly, unobtrusively, uncritically, without pride or boast, I take my stand with *that* testimony. With malice toward none and with charity toward all, we have stepped outside the traditional church to stand with the organic expression of the body of Christ.

Christendom is basically a great organization, or should I say a group of organizations. Most of it is in a situation not too unlike the ancient Hebrew faith. The Waldensian Christians (who bore

101

the torch so valiantly during the dark ages) like the Hebrews, were once the very center of the work of God on the earth. Today, they are an empty shell, a religious organization with the sign "church" hung around its neck. So, too, the Roman Catholics, the Lutherans, the Anabaptists, the United Brethren, and on and on. Wouldn't it be wonderful, if once God was through with a people, they could just slip off the pages of history and vanish. Instead, the bones go on walking long after the spirit is gone.

I have made a few simple points. We have seen the origin of chain-of-command type organization. It was for angels. One angel, Lucifer, seeks to weave all men into that organizational web. Further, the church is not an organization but a living organism. Most entities called "church" are simply religious organizations set in the structure of ancient Rome, Assyria, and Babylon. Most of the Christian family is in a religious system, one appallingly similar—in set-up—to the world system itself.

Just in case there still happens to be a doubter or two sitting our there on the back row, let me call secular history to the witness stand once more and ask if Christendom is a religious system. Let history witness to the truth of those statements. Here are a few excerpts from Durant's mammoth eleven volume, *Story of Civilization*. These quotations are all taken from volume three, *Caesar and Christ*. Read. And weep.

On Roman Organization:
"Rome has had no rival in the art of government . . . . within that unsurpassed framework Rome built a culture Greek in origin . . .; she absorbed with appreciation, and preserved with tenacity, the technical, intellectual, and artistic heritage that she had received from Carthage and Egypt, Greece and the East." [3]

On Paganism's Triumph Over the Church:
"When Christianity conquered Rome, the ecclesiastical structure of [paganism], the title and vestments of the pontifex maximus, *the worship*

---

[3] Durant, *The Story of Civilization*, volume III, pg. 670-671.

of Great Mother . . . passed like maternal blood into the new religion, and captive Rome captured her conqueror. "[4]

On Church Structure:

"The reins and skills of government were handed down by a dying empire to a viriler papacy. . . ."[5]

On Constantine's "conversion" to Christianity:

"Was his conversion sincere . . . or a consummate stroke of political wisdom? Probably the latter. . . . In his Gallic court he had surrounded himself with pagan scholars and philosophers. . . . Throughout his reign he treated the bishops as his political aides. . . . Christianity was to him a means, not an end. . . . Their teachers had inculcated submission to the civil powers. . . . Constantine aspired to an absolute monarchy; such a government would profit from religious support. . . the Church seemed to offer a spiritual correlate for monarchy. "[6]

On the Paganizing of Church Order:

"It was not merely that the Church took over some religious customs . . . the stole and other vestments of pagan priests, the use of incense and holy water . . . the burning of candles . . . the worship of saints, the architecture . . . the law of Rome as a basis for [Church law], the title . . . Supreme Pontiff . . . . The Roman gift was above all a vast framework of government, which . . . became the structure of ecclesiastical rule [!!!]. The Roman Church followed in the footsteps of the Roman state . . . . As Judea had given Christianity ethics . . . so now Rome gave it organization . . . . "[7]

Now, my question: Shall we be part of organized religion?

Well, someone may disagree with my interpretation of the *spiritual* origin of organization. And I might be wrong (perish the thought!). But secular history is in agreement: present day Christianity is organized! Organized in the image of Rome, who was organized in the image of Darius I, Ol' Superpagan! Now,

---

[4] Ibid., pg. 670-671.
[5] Ibid., pg. 671-672.
[6] Ibid., pg. 655-656.
[7] Ibid., pg. 618-619.

dear brother, do you really believe that when God gave to us this glorious creature called the church that the Almighty, Living God took His cue from Darius and gave *her* an organizational structure made in the image of Babylon and Persia?

No, everything in us tells us the church of the first century must have been radically different in function from anything else on earth: she, forever a-organizational. Our mission? To get back to that organic, innate, natural unstructured expression of the church.

I know not what course other men may choose, dear reader, but for me and my house . . . we are going back to the ways, not of Rome, but of the early church.

Would you dare secede to a lesser mission?

Quo Vadis?

Now, I would like to draw some conclusions based on the facts we have just viewed.

First, church life cannot survive in an organizational structure. Part of our task on earth is to see a clear restoring of the experience of church life upon the earth. We must not get organized. Church life must flourish on the earth again.

Second, the religious system has consistently given a hard time to those groups of Christians *outside* the system. This has been true in all countries and in all ages where Christian groups outside the system have existed. Be it Islam, Buddhism, Hinduism, organized Judaism or organized Christianity . . . at the very least, it is the tendency of religious organizations to oppose Christians who refuse to organize. We should not be surprised if such should be our lot at some future date.

Third, we cannot get totally outside the sphere of the world system. The world system covers the earth. Our only hope of getting totally away from it would be to move to the mountains— or desert—and become hermits. In regard to the world system, this is our call: to be *in* the world, yet not *of* the world. But there is one system inside the world system we should stay as far away from as we can get: we should stay out of the *religious system*. Not help it, not feed it, not encourage it—yet not fight it, either. Just ignore it.

Perhaps the best illustration of this is compacted into the first ten verses of Daniel 6.

This passage clearly states that by this organizational pattern all Babylon was ruled. Verses 1 to 3 give us a perfect description of chain-of-command. These same three verses show us Daniel's perfect willingness to find secular employment right in the middle of the organizational structure. But there was one department within this structure which Daniel had nothing to do with, and would not go along with . . . he would not conform, in any way, and change he would not . . . even it if meant having to give up his bedroom and sleep with lions!

So, as we learned in vacation Bible school when we were only seven years old, come what may, let us dare to be a Daniel!

Fourth, if the religious system should ever oppose us—if we face our own modern version of "dangers from the Jews"—we must have the same attitude, outlook and response that Paul had.

A Test

I would like to end this point by a reference to the future. Man in his fallen state is *naturally,* organically pagan. Works of God down through the ages eventually revert to the ways of fallen man. How can we know for sure when we have arrived at such a state?

How can we know when the Lord is through with us? Frankly, I haven't any idea. Here are some possibilities . . . . When *these* things have become definite trends among us: Perhaps when we have become institutionalized . . . owning permanent property. When we become worldly . . . again. (Please remember, we *were* in the world, we gave up the world; we can easily go back.) When we leave Christ as the center of our message. When the Bible, or evangelism, or morality or "the church" becomes our center.

When we cease experiencing the Lord, and only talk about experiencing Him. When we stop being seekers. When we become sectarian. When we fight one another. When we take a list like this and stuff it down one another's throats with half a dozen possible interpretations of its meaning. I don't have any idea if *those* are signs or not that the Lord has moved away.

But there are two possibilities I would like to definitely list: (1) When we *start* fellowshipping with the religious system it will be time for us to fold up our tent and steal off the stage of history. (2) When we *stop* being open to, when we stop fellowshipping with individual Christians in that system . . . then it will be time to close shop and vanish from the earth.

It seems impossible to have nothing to do with the religious system and be totally open to all Christians. Yet, we must. This is our call. Dear brother, or sister, whatever our future, whatever our lot, please hold before you the example of Paul under pressure from the Jews. Make this your conduct.

CHAPTER 9

Our Relationship to Individual Christians

Now we come to a totally different subject. We have talked about our relationship to "the Jew" and to "the gentile," but what of our relationship to individual Christians in the religious system? Answering this question poses a tremendous problem. Many times the Scripture can help us and guide us through the problems we face; either by a direct word or by some example. But not here! We face a problem here that was simply unknown in the first century. Christians were in the church . . . that is, in church life. They were not also in a half dozen *other* religious movements. Today the reverse is true. Almost no Christians are in the experience of church life; virtually all devout Christians are very involved in one or more religious institutions. We have a big problem, and no Scriptural parallel to guide us. Just glance at the unique situation we face.

Today most Christians have never experienced church life, or rather . . . have never even heard of church life. "Church"—to most believers of today—is a building, and "church life" would mean (if you made them guess) the two to five hours per week they spend at that building.

The more devout believer today is probably (or tries to be) a participating member of the "church building" and also a member of one or *more* interdenominational organizations.

Now, none of this mentality existed in the first century. There existed no such thing as believers *in* the religious system (and *not* in the experience of the church) as over against those who were not in the religious system (and who *were* in the daily experience of the church).

Let me try to illustrate just how far afield the present day Christian mentality is from a first century mentality. If you went to Thessalonica, you would find saints who gathered in Jason's home. You might find a few staying home, and you might even find some who had forsaken the faith and who could have gone back to worshipping idols in the pagan temples.

But you didn't find a dozen interdenominational organizations, three ministerial associations and 144 denominations; seventy-five independent "churches," thirty home-Bible study groups, ten "half-way houses," and three "church-in-the-home" organizations. Such a situation simply never existed in the first century.

Problems they had a-plenty. But the above were *not* on the list.

So the question remains unresolved: What shall be our relationship to Christians who are totally immersed in organized religion? The problem almost defies solution. Whatever our response to this problem, it had better be high. Why? Because the situation demands it.

Our Present Mentality

What is the difference between our mentality and the first century mentality? I am not speaking of doctrine; I am not speaking of beliefs; I am not speaking of our practice . . . in fact, I am not even referring to anything we are consciously aware of. It is an outlook, an environmental attitude. And in a way, this "modern Christian mentality" exerts more influence on the way you do things than all of your doctrines and all of your methods, goals, dreams, visions, and hopes combined.

Today there is a mentality that equates a non-profit interdenominational organization with the church. A man-made organization having equal billing with God's very purpose for creation! Unbelievable.

And this is not a deliberately thought-out attitude. The thing just hangs there in the atmosphere . . . unseen, unthought, unnoticed . . . but so powerfully present and so incredibly influential.

The same is true with division in the body of Christ. This is an age that lauds division. Of course none of us thinks of it that way. Let me illustrate.

A fine, spiritual brother gathers a group of businessmen together. He shares his vision for a new organization . . . one that will do something unique . . . something needed. The men present catch his vision. They applaud his daring . . . and *another* severing of the Lord's body occurs. Division is praiseworthy!

That is an unquestioned mentality of our day. A triple-digit number of churches in one city . . . outnumbering gas stations! Interdenominational organizations and "store fronts" are proliferating, home Bible studies and "churches-in-the-home" are multiplying like taxes!!!

And organizations! The Christian faith is out hunting for men with great organizational gifts. Men who can whip together a clean, slick, efficient organization . . . one that gets the job done . . . for the Lord. As I stated previously, some of the great denominations boast in their intricate, smooth-running, super-efficient organizational operation.

All this is an unspoken, unthought mentality that elevates a "thing" to the level of a "person." The Lord's church is a woman; a living, breathing, divine organism. An organization is a cold, sterile, man-conceived contraption. Yet our mentality today unwittingly exalts the "thing" above the wife of God!!!

I have no bone to pick with anyone on this subject. What I have described is simply the status quo. This is the way things are. And we've got to learn to live in this age the way things are. They will not change . . . not in your lifetime. The question before us is this: "With the situation the way it is, how do we relate to other believers?" This is a hard question. Be careful. We *must* find the highest possible way. Whatever that way is, it will not be an easy way, because we are surrounded by a Christian mentality so utterly far afield of the first century outlook.

Frankly, I sometimes envy our first century brothers. Yes, they had lots of problems. Yes, they suffered a lot. But they had some things going for them, too. They had *scriptural* problems. But us? We have so many problems that aren't even scriptural! Just think of all the problems they *didn't* have!!!

The Two Mentalities Contrasted

I'd like to describe what the first century church might have looked like if they had been blessed(!) with our mentality. But that would take a book. Instead, just for a moment, let's see the contrast between these two mentalities.

Let's say you got saved in the first century . . . in the city of Iconium . . . a gentile church which was raised up by Paul. You had two choices: meet with the other believers in your city . . . or forget the whole thing. Those were your *only* two choices. Simple enough!

There was one group of Christians in Iconium. One. That was all. No place else for you to go. Not another "church" meeting down the way. No interdenominational organization you could join to "devote your God-given talents to." No independent worker sailing through town with a lot of great stories to entertain you with for the evening down at the local amphitheater.

Nope. Not a dozen churches. Not a dozen works, or workers or Christian organizations to choose from. One church. One people. (How dull.) No choices. Nothing else. Not even a mentality that could conceive of such a choice, or of division.

No "Slums for Christ." No house for Athenian hippies. No "Mission to Israel." Not even a campus non-profit organization to win the local "Aristotelian philosophy students to Christ." No "Rancho del Cristo," no "Vegetarians for Christ;" not even a summer retreat grounds, no interdenominational tract society. Imagine: no Bible schools, no Christian colleges, no "International Corinthian Charismatic Fellowship." No "Marketplace Mission." No Christian coffee house, no missionary effort for the gentile

110

lepers in South-southeast Ethiopia. And not even a healing service down at the Garbanzo Room in the Iconium Hilton.

Nothing in Iconium but the church, and only *one* of those.

What's my point? This: There were no Christians in the religious system in Iconium. The Christians were all to be found in one place and one place only: in the body of Christ—which gathered in unbroken unity—in Iconium. The church was the sole repository of Christians in the city of Iconium. There were non-believers. Jewish non-believers. You could find them down at the local synagogue. There were gentile non-believers. You could locate them down at any one of the nearby temples, bowing before some goddess.

Non-believers were to be found in two religious systems: Judaism and paganism. Believers were to be found in one place: in the organic, daily life of the bride of Jesus Christ.

Imagine. The thought had not yet been born on this planet—not even dreamed in a dream—that it was possible for a local body of believers to experience division!

Once more, think of all the things first century believers didn't have in their city.

There was no chaos: some Christians meeting in homes, others at the synagogue . . . another group that rented out the local pagan temple every Sunday morning.

No interdenominational organization with president, board of directors and staff, with a large building just off the market square, writing out in longhand and rolling up little scrolls to pass out to (of all people!) all the Christians in the city . . . to raise enough money to send brother Apollos to Babylon.

No traveling band of young troubadors holding forth in the local arena, all wearing identical white-with-golden-trim tunics . . . singing psalms to the tune of some of the latest pagan songs, giving their testimony of how wonderful it is to live by faith . . . just before they whip out the "love offering" sack. (That distant noise you just heard was Paul rolling over in his grave.) Yes, the early believers had some very distinct advantages going for them.

Christians, generally, were in the church. There was no

division. To be saved and in the fellowship of the local body of believers was to be *outside* the religious system.

True, you might find a backslidden Christian back in the synagogue (if Jewish) or in a pagan temple (if gentile). But you didn't find a whole room full of them *meeting* in the pagan temple and calling it "the second Iconium church" . . . or "Pagan Temples for Christ, International."

Today the situation is reversed. The Christian faith has taken organizational systematization upon itself . . . and most of the Lord's people are in that religious organizational structure. And we, I repeat, have got a first class problem—a problem not found in Scripture.

To complicate the problem even more, the Lord's people don't know all this. They haven't the cloudiest notion that they belong to a structured organization that someone has glued the title "assembly" or "church" onto.

Anyway, you get the idea; the present day Christian mentality is a set thing; an unconscious thing; and we have to live with it . . . despite the fact it is both universally adhered to and at the same time, totally opposed to the mentality and outlook of first century believers.

Our Attitude?

Now to the big problem. A gigantic problem. What shall be our relationship to Christians in the religious system? Remember, there are dear, precious Christians in the religious system. And remember this; they don't have even a translucent notion that they are|in a system.

My dear old grandmother was just about as devout a church member as a human could be. Now if you had told Granny that her denomination was an organization . . . and that organization was patterned after the structure of the Roman Empire, which had been borrowed from Babylon, which was a replica of angelic order,

112

chaired by Lucifer, she might have either fainted dead away or possibly chased you out of the house.

She didn't know that. She wouldn't agree that it was true, wouldn't have wanted to know it if it was, wouldn't have changed if she had known! That's just information Granny would do better without.

Not everyone will leave . Not everyone wants to!

A few will seek a way out. A few will leave. Most will not. Please remember that.

Now get a firm fix on this: There is a vast difference between the religious system and the dear, precious saints of God—some in love with the Lord with all their hearts—who are in that system. These people are as precious to God as we are to Him, perhaps more precious . . . under less scrutiny and judgment than we are. You are not loved by the Lord more than they! Nor am I!

Now we come to our calling. What shall be our relationship to the Lord's people in the system? This is our mission . . . the Lord has called us to the impossible. You see, if we have nothing to do with other Christians, we will end up bigots. *That* will destroy us. It should. On the other hand, if we have anything to do with that *system* they are in, we will end up back in it, too! And that will also destroy us.

The Lord has called us to an impossible position.

We must leave that system. Leave it. Never go back to it. Despise it; never help it, condone it, participate in it, nor even touch it . . . and at the very same moment, we must be totally open to the Christians in it. An impossible call.

To leave the system, yet be as open, as undemanding, as guileless, as uncritical, as patient, as unconditional in our love as we are toward the saints we live with daily in the practice of church life. This is impossible; it can't be done. Nevertheless, it *must* be done!

I'm not hedging this statement. It is unequivocal. We must see other Christians as the dearest people on earth, not one atom less wonderful than the dearest saint in this part of the body of Christ you now fellowship with and whom you love so unreservedly.

How can we do this? The answer will not be easy to find. Perhaps it won't be found (I remind you, we are dealing with an unscriptural problem. Scripturally, all Christians ought to be outside the systematization of organized religion.)

We have one thing going for us, though. To a large extent, our problems are nonexistent. Most Christians "out there" are monumentally uninterested in us. When they hear about us, they are underwhelmed. We are easily overlooked. We are a very forgettable people. What do I mean?

Basically, it is only the seeker, the heart-hungry Christian, and the recently saved "gentile" who never so much as heard of Christianity or the system, who make up our ranks. The rest of the Christian family is some way able to not even see us.

Nonetheless, you must never say anything negative about other Christians; never compare other Christians to "us." There is no "them" or "us." All believers are as dear in God's sight as a Paul or a Peter or a John. Some of the Lord's people in the system are among the dearest Christians in the world. Let this be your standard: When you meet a Christian in the religious system, treat him as we treat one another! Greet him with all the love and openness of unhindered hearts.

On the other hand, we do have a task, and we must not get distracted. And that just might create a problem. He will love your openness; it is only logical he will try to get you involved in his religious activities.

So be sure, one day you will wake up and find yourself in a tight spot. One day, with all this uninhibited openness on your part, you are going to get invited to a fund-raising banquet . . . or something! THEN you are going to have a problem.

And what will you do?

As I said, you've got *yourself* a problem! Sorry. There are few guidelines anyone can offer you.

Let's sum up.

As to the religious system: In the days of Paul, there existed a religious system. Paul grew up in that system, but he left it when he became a believer. That system persecuted him . . . all his life. He never went back into that systematization. And that system

114

never got into the body of Christ. Paul and Judaism were two worlds apart.

Today the situation is radically changed. We became a Christian only to discover that virtually all believers are in a religious system. We have been called to come out of that system . . . and yet be totally one with the believers who are in it. Impossible. But, still we must.

Further, we can expect some opposition from that system. History says so. We must never react to that opposition, or in any way be negatively affected by it . . . and we must continue to be totally open to all saints .

Brother, take the Christ deposited in you and share *him* with the saint you are with.

One last word about fellowshipping with individual Christians in organized Christianity: When you are with them, put out of your mind any of the experiences or "light" you feel you might have that they don't. Such an attitude is located very near the taproot of a sectarian spirit. (The taproot itself is *pride!*) Just be an ordinary brother. Most of all, lay aside all remembrance of the massive perverseness of the present day mess we Christians have inherited from our forefathers. Conduct yourself as though the church still knew the unity she did in each city some two milleniums ago.

Every day my attitude—the attitude of my heart—must be this: There has been no division in the body of Christ. We are all still one. There is only one church in this city . . . locatable, visible, attendable. We all meet, we are all one. We love one another unhindered and unconditionally; and the believers meet in perfect harmony. This must be our mentality.

This may not be the situation. But this must be our attitude, our vantage point. It is from this lookout station alone that we must view all things.

Back to the last point. Know this: When another Christian sees your friendliness, he is going to invite you to something in that system he is in. And then it is you who are going to face some thorny problems. But you will just have to have those problems, for this openness to Christians and closedness to institutionalized religion . . . is part of our mission.

In every such situation, you are going to have to take this matter to the Lord. We will each have to individually deal with the Lord concerning these situations. The very basis of our old nature must be rooted out. In every man, there is a sectarian spirit . . . longing to be expressed. And contrariwise, there is also part of each of us that would dearly like to go back to Babylon. Both elements must be dealt with.

We are called to be a people without a sectarian spirit . . . and to be *out* of the religious system. An impossible call. I suspect that such a people are extinct today. Yet *this* is our goal. The accomplishment of it will be a divine event.

May we see such a high mission . . . accomplished.

CHAPTER 10

The World System

Paul spoke of another danger: the gentiles. Let us look at this crisis also.

We pointed out, at the beginning, that the world system in its simplest term is local government. A more complete view would say "the gentile world is all of organized secular society."

In our day, here in America, there are few, if any, dangers from the gentiles . . . from local government. But in other nations there are dangers: from the Chinese government, from the Spanish government, from the government of Saudi Arabia, or Afghanistan. These are the dangers from the *gentiles*.

Let's chronicle Paul's run-ins with "the gentiles." It is Paul who illustrates to us so clearly the standard by which we should live in the midst of a gentile-controlled world. Paul did not find it easy "to be in the world, but not of the world." Behold what the gentiles did to him!

1. Early Christian Years.

Damascus, Syria. Paul left by the unorthodox means of "over-the-wall-in-a-basket" because of the local government's plot to kill him.

2. First Trip.

(1)*Pisidian-Antioch.* The Jews were jealous, but it was mainly the leading gentiles whom they stirred up that drove Paul out of the city.

(2)*Iconium.* The disbelieving Jews stirred up the gentiles. It was embittered gentiles and their rulers who led the attempted mistreatment and the attempted stoning.

(3)*Lystra.* The Jews from Antioch and Iconium were definitely the culprits, but the multitudes of the city (the gentiles) turned out to be the ones who did the actual stoning.

3. Second Trip.

(1)*Philippi.* Here the gentiles did it all. (The city was virtually devoid of Jews.) The trial, the beating, the imprisonment were all at the hands of the gentiles.

(2)*Thessalonica.* The Jews stirred up the mob and set the city in an uproar, but it was the gentile rulers who hauled Jason to the court and the local gentile government which banished Paul.

(3)*Berea.* The Thessalonian Jews did the instigating, but it was the agitated gentile crowds that caused Paul to flee the city.

(4)*Corinth.* A host of Jews rose up against Paul and brought him to the gentile "judgment seat."

4. Third Trip.

Ephesus. The gentiles, led by Demetrius, were the ones who brought Paul's four-year stay in that area of Asia Minor to an end.

5. Later.

Jerusalem. The gentile soldiers saved Paul's life, but he spent two years imprisoned in Caesarea as a result. It was to a gentile court in Rome that he was sent to be tried, and finally, it was the gentiles *alone* (utterly unprovoked by any Jewish hand) who beheaded Paul.[1]

I have listed some of the persecutions Paul knew at the hands of the gentiles in order to ask a question: In the light of all that unfair abuse, what was Paul's attitude toward the gentiles?

Or better, what was Paul's attitude toward the world system?

---

[1] *It is interesting to note that down through the 1900 years of church history, it is "the Jews"—the religious element of society—who do most of the persecuting, but it is ultimately "the gentiles"—the secular element—who do the killing! The gentiles are usually the ones who annihilate the work of God. Out of hundreds of*

Our Attitude Towards Worldliness

Paul carried two relationships toward the world. As far as "worldliness" . . . Paul forsook the world. As far as the world's persecution of him, well . . . we will look at that point more closely in just a moment.

Let's look at the first point. What shall be our attitude toward the "worldliness" of the world system?

We will begin here to seek and find a standard to which we can all aspire.

You can do three things with the attractiveness of the world: (1) Give yourself to it, (2) forsake it, or (3) camp somewhere between these two points. (You can compromise.)

Every one of you wishes to forsake the world. Wonderful. Then let us drop the other two possibilities. Still, that brings up a problem. What does "forsake"mean? I wish to remind you that "forsake" has a very anemic blood count in our age. To totally forsake the world is a thing rarely seen in *any* age . . . certainly in *this* one.

Let's say you *do* forsake the world . . . truly get past today's ways and into something meaningful. The great divorce. Now you have arrived at the second great problem.

"What will now be my attitude toward the world, and worldly people and worldly things?" You could get an extra-long nose from which to look down on people. You could get a monk's robe— or a nun's habit—to call attention to your divestation.

There is something else you can do: Go get a two-bladed axe and spend the rest of your life attacking the world, worldliness and those in the world. "Get out of the world, like me," can become your center.

---

possible examples, here is one: The Little Flock received unrelenting opposition from the religious system . . . especially the Christian missionaries . . . . They were hardly ever bothered by the "gentiles." But in the end, it was Communism that unsheathed the blade—that is, it was the "gentiles" who stopped the Little Flock in China. The missionaries and the institutional church persecuted them, but the secular government stopped them.

Looking through church history, you quickly see that most believers who divest themselves of the world end up self-righteous. So here are some possibilities: (1) Be worldly, (2) compromise, or (3) leave the world. If you choose the last category, you still have choices: (1) Be self-righteous and proud of what you've done; (2) attack the system and those who don't leave it.

Some go farther, not only attacking and deriding the world and trying to get others to "do exactly like I do, believe like me, dress like me," but also turning bitter and even cynical toward the world.

Well, all of the above attitudes are pretty immature, and you can spot them easily. If we are to see the banner moved up that mountain, we must find a new, higher attitude toward a world we have left behind us.

I want us to be an unworldly people; as much out of it as possible while still being on the same planet with it, and having to make our living in the midst of it. But what about *after* the break? Let's say you break with worldliness as much as the ancient Franciscan monks once tried to do. What kind of person will you become *after* that?

Let This Be Our Standard

I would commend to you this standard: Get out of the systematization the world has put mankind into. Break loose . . . utterly, totally, finally . . . forever. Even at the cost of losing all worldly possessions for all the rest of your life.

Then, having left it, guard against all pride. Neither boast nor attack. Don't make a career of telling others what you've done, and by all means do not spend the rest of your life attacking worldliness.

Finally, having broken with the world, I implore you, do not push your standard off on *anyone* else. For instance, some new brother who just drove into town last night in his gold chariot, dragging his color TV, silk shirts, and three-deck yacht behind him. Let him be. His conduct is of no concern to you. Don't impose your walk on him. What each of us does, we should do because we are by love compelled—*not* by another brother compelled.

By the way, if you happen to be someone who just galloped into town on a gold chariot, I can pretty well guarantee you that a young saint who has been here—oh, less than a year—will probably meet you at the door saying some pretty awful, lawful things. Be careful . . . even if he stands on your chest, don't get upset. Expect this kind of thing. It will happen.

Our Attitude Towards a World System that Persecutes

I'd like to move now to our second relationship to the world system. The world system—that is, the unbeliever, or more specifically, the gentile government—often persecutes the Lord's people. What is the proper conduct of a believer during such an hour of persecution?

I would like to call upon the life of Paul of Tarsus to be our example once more. Paul walked around on this earth seemingly oblivious to what people did to him. It was almost like those cataclysmic events never happened. He forgot his past . . . fast. This is a virtue not found in most of the Lord's servants.

It is not what men do to us that tries our beings . . . destroying us or transforming us. It is not their action; it is our re-action that tests the mettle. I talked to you earlier about "a little man down inside you" who wants to defend himself. Well, he has a twin brother. There is another little fellow down inside you who wants to be persecuted . . . so he can tell ("brag" is a better word) about it. I have a sneaking suspicion that there are brothers here who are itching to bring a message someday which they can entitle "The Day I Was Persecuted by the World System"!

By the way, I am aware that there are also brothers in this room with the very opposite problem. You'd walk all the way around the world backwards to avoid a confrontation or a pressure situation. Some way, dear saints, both these attitudes fall wide of the mark. I trust we will—as a people—be neither of these. Wishing to be persecuted—wishing to flee all pressure situations no matter what . . . these two extremes must both go.

Do you wish to get persecuted? Think about it. Do you revel in it? I know that when the church is on the offensive, or undergoing an assault, or when the church is really in a season of victorious conquest, invariably some brother or sister comes down with this syndrome. I'll not scotch that. All I can say is, don't condone such an outlook. A persecution complex must never take root in the church. Don't take out adoption papers on such an attitude.

We must some way learn to march forward, in dangerous places, with a bold, uncompromising gospel . . . unafraid. Yet we must never revel in opposition. If persecution comes, let it; but as quickly as possible, let it also *pass on* . . . without comment. Order your life as though it never happened.

Just as a side observation, please be aware that sometimes we do appear just a teensie-weensie bit peculiar! Airport meetings, street marches, etc. To us this all seems perfectly normal. But to others, maybe we should realize that we may look just ever-so-slightly odd. We are bound to stir up just a few adverse reactions. When they come, be slow to respond. Do not seize these slight antagonisms to get "persecuted for the Lord."

If ever the "gentiles" turn the malicious side toward you, treat it as though it never happened. Like Paul, you never saw it, you never heard it, but most of all . . . *you never felt it.*

I'd like to sum up.

Leave worldliness. Utterly. As few people in church history ever have. Having done so, do not be proud, do not make a career out of attacking worldliness. And *do not* try to get anyone else to conform to your standard.

Secondly, when the world system (the gentiles) gives us difficulty, treat these incidents as though they never happened. Do not cultivate a persecution complex. Yet, let us be a bold people . . .

122

for we are taking the Gospel to a world which is a little less than enthusiastic about Jesus Christ . . . and/or His church.

There is little chance of overt danger from civil authorities in North America or in Northern Europe. (This is not true in Southern and Eastern Europe.) In most of the rest of the world there really is danger of physical harm from "the gentiles." If outright physical persecution from civil authorities should ever be our lot, what shall be our outlook? Well, let us take the standard raised by Paul, the world's leading authority on being persecuted by civil powers.

Paul States His Attitude Towards an Empire that Persecuted Him

Paul tells us clearly his attitude toward the gentile government that has persecuted him so harshly. He does so in two letters. Which Letters? Romans and Titus. Let us look at those books and what they say.

First, Romans. Do you recall, a little earlier, my telling the story of how Paul faced death getting out of Ephesus? It was there in Ephesus that Demetrius led a riot against Paul. It was in this setting that Paul wrote II Corinthians. He managed to get out of the city and eventually he got to Corinth. All during this part of his journey the Jews were everywhere, plotting to kill him.

It was in Corinth that a religious order of fanatical Jews called Daggermen made their boldest attempt to assassinate Paul. It was also at this time, in fact it happened in every place Paul stopped, that a mounting witness of warnings kept coming to him: "Do not go to Jerusalem." Paul knew he probably faced certain death on his trip to Jerusalem. He could plainly tell he would probably never see those twelve gentile churches again and he would never see Rome, or personally minister to the church in Rome.

He had once thought his second letter to Corinth (written from Ephesus) might be his last. Now—as he pens a letter to the saints in Rome (from Corinth)—he is virtually sure *this will be his last* written word.

He talked about "the Jews" in this letter. Remember? But he also talked about "the gentiles." Just before you read this passage, go back a few pages and look at that list of what "the gentiles" had done to Paul.

Alright, now read what Paul writes about these rascals—the gentiles—in his letter to Rome.

Remember, these lines are written by a man who fled civil authorities in Damascus, a man pushed out of Pisidian-Antioch and Iconium by them . . . by a man stoned virtually to death in Lystra, by a man beaten half to death by them in Philippi and several other undesignated places . . . written by a man who was banished by them from the city of Thessalonica.

Listen, as Paul writes from Corinth, where he had once been hauled before the gentile judgment seat. Paul, too, is writing to the Roman Christians, some of whom only a few years before had been banished from this city by an edict of the Emperor.

Read this incredible passage. He is writing about "the gentiles," the civil authorities. who have frequently fallen just short of killing him!

Let every person be in subjection to the governing authorities. For there is no authority except from God, and those which exist are established by God. Therefore, he who resists authority has opposed the ordinance of God; and they who have opposed will receive condemnation upon themselves. For rulers are not a cause of fear for good behavior, but for evil. Do you want to have no fear of authority? Do what is good, and you will have praise from the same; for it is a minister of God to you for good. But if you do what is evil, be afraid; for it does not bear the sword for nothing; for it is a minister of God, an avenger who brings wrath upon the one who practices evil. Wherefore it is necessary to be in subjection, not only because of wrath, but also for conscience' sake. For because of this, you also pay taxes, for rulers are servants of God, devoting themselves to this very thing. Render to all what is due them: Tax to whom tax is due; custom to whom custom; fear to whom fear; honor to whom honor.

Romans 13:1-7

I believe this passage speaks for itself. *This* was the attitude Paul had toward the gentiles, *after* nearly two decades of facing death at their hands . . . times without number.

124

But if those words are remarkable, wait until you see the backdrop for the next scene.

The second letter in which Paul refers to "the gentiles" is Titus. This is a letter written years *after* he penned the letter to Rome. Maybe we had better stop right here and explain that Paul did *not* die at the end of his third journey, contrary to what he expected. He escaped the Jews . . . he was not killed by the Daggermen or any other part of the religious system. Here is the story.

Paul got to Jerusalem . . . alive. But he was almost killed in a riot there; it was a riot provoked by "the Jews." He was rescued, interestingly enough, by "the gentiles!" But that moment is a watershed moment in Paul's life. That will be the last known time Paul ever actually faced death at the hands of religious man. From now on it will be only "the gentile" who will physically harm him.

Paul ends up in jail in Caesarea for two years. Probably the only reason he was there so long was that his keepers were hoping to get a bribe out of him; there appears to be no other possible justification for his long imprisonment. Then there was approximately one more year—as a prisoner—he spent en route to Rome. Then he spent two years as a prisoner *in* Rome. He was waiting in line there for a brief interview with Nero.

Eventually Paul was released. He does not know it, but he has only a few years left to live. (Unknown to him, death by the blade awaits him in Rome . . . at the hands of the gentiles.) Anyway, one of the things he did during this brief release was to make a circuit tour of the island of Crete with Titus. Paul then leaves Titus and goes to a city called Nicopolis. There he writes Titus a letter. Once again, after all the imprisonment, beatings, abuses, unfair treatment, dishonesties and even an attempt by a governor to get a bribe from him, Paul restates the view he earlier propounded in the letter to Rome. The man has not changed. No bitterness has entered his soul. For all the world you would never know the man had ever suffered anything at the hands of the gentiles. Certainly you would never guess that the writer of this book had recently spent five years in jail—unjustly—at the hands of civil authorities.

Remind them to be subject to rulers, to authorities, to be obedient, to be ready for every good deed. . . . Titus 3:1

What shall be our attitude toward the world system . . . toward *the gentile?* Look up, and see at what heights that original standard was first raised. Our attitude, our outlook, our *re*action, our walk must be not one mite lower than that set by that servant of God named Paul, who was the most persecuted mortal who lived in all the first century.

Who knows what nations we might one day find ourselves in, and what trials and tests might await us. We may one day learn that this . . . suffering—with nobility—at the hands of *the gentiles,* . . . is also *our* mission!

Part Three

CHAPTER 11

The Standard of the Worker

Now we must look in on a totally different subject . . . the man who serves God . . . the gifted man . . . call him Apostle, prophet, evangelist or whatever. I shall refer to him as worker. This man is the builder. Yet he is the tearer-downer, too! He brings more divisions and problems, breaks more hearts, causes more grief, destroys more lives, than all the other believers in history combined. Peevish, picky, legalistic, suspicious of others, super-guardian of his own work, hypercritical of everyone else . . . he is, hands down, the worst blot on any page of church history. Frightening, isn't it?

"With a track record like that, let's get rid of the whole lot. Out with the workers!" Well, sorry to say, as destructive as he is, the worker is essential. By God's own very special choice, the worker is the one ordered to establish the church here on earth. He is the most needed element in the building of the Kingdom of God. But a true and faithful worker, who can find him?

It is not the position of the worker that is in question. It is the *quality* of the man that is so horrifying.

A new standard among workers is needed. In fact, a whole new breed of workers is needed; perhaps the single most needed element in the future work of God here on earth is this: a new breed of workers.

Let's talk a little about the worker. The WORKER! The source of *all* problems in church history. Look at his conduct. *There* is the problem. What is needed? A new standard of conduct needs to be raised; a standard higher than any seen in a *group* of men in centuries.

What I speak of needs to be seen with the deepest eyes . . . the deepest eyes of your spirit; it must arrest you, even scare you!

A new breed of workers, a new standard of the worker established by a new breed of men. Let me pause and say that in the strictest view, there should be no such thing as a "standard for the worker." The standard of a worker's life should be no higher than the standard for all of us who believe. Please remember that what I say of the worker fits every saint in the church.

Two comments are in order. On this subject we need a revelation, not an understanding. Secondly, don't *you* ever seek to be a worker. The Lord will do what He will do. You can't stop the fire in your heart or the gift in your being if the Lord has put it there. It will come. If you are, you are; if you are not, you are not. "But shouldn't we seek the highest gift? Aren't we told to do this?" Sure. But that gift is love. Seek love!

Now, concerning conduct. Paul said, "Imitate me." That's amazing. Paul invited men to imitate him. How daring, and how dangerous. What a man to dare give such an invitation.

Let me explain why his invitation is so dangerous. Someone once said to me, "Did you ever notice that we Christians imitate the Christian leaders whom we admire? But have you noticed that, invariably, it is their *weaknesses* we imitate!" And it's true! Too true!

Knowing this from the very outset, I have implored Christians close to me to not imitate me; don't imitate my peculiarities, my eccentricities; don't imitate my weaknesses. Imitating these oddities doesn't make you spiritual. The cross makes you spiritual. Pain is the cause of spiritual growth, not the peculiarities of an earthen vessel. My peculiarities will not add one hair to your spiritual height.

132

You might be interested to know that when I began ministering among you an epidemic of "Southern drawl" broke out. You don't need to be told where that came from. Gratefully, that stage passed. The longer we know one another the less this happens.

This business of young men imitating the worker sure puts an awesome responsibility on the worker. If he is loved and admired, he will be imitated. But the *most* imitated part will be his weaknesses . . . his spiritual weaknesses! Point: He'd better not have any.

I realize that is more or less impossible. But it still must be the goal.

You may never know what a man is like, even if you work side by side with him for years. You may *never* know the real inside of a man. But that is not true of a worker. You will know him. How? Simple. At the end of five or ten or twelve years, take a look at his work ... and by seeing it, you can know the man. By that time (but not before that time, for it takes that long for the imprint to be made), the work will be in the image of the man. Point: If this be true, then the worker had better be in the image of his Lord.

You may come to a group of Christians who are standing as the church in the city where they gather. (I am talking obviously about a work that would be *outside* the religious system.) You visit awhile. You come to love and admire the worker, but you are horrified at the work. But be sure, the work is a magnification of the man. On the other hand, you may love the work and be very impressed with its depth, and at the same time dislike the worker. But, in fact, they are the same. The man may look and act one way and the church another, but they are inseparable. Look at the work the end of ten years, and you will know the worker. I am not speaking of the size of the work, but the image — the personality, the depth — of the work.

The true nature of the inward parts of the worker can be seen his work. Be sure that, after about seven years it becomes possible to totally hide this fact.

Therefore, you had better be about the business of knowing

nothing but Jesus Christ. If you get up, walk around, breathe and talk for seven years, and know something other than Christ, that "something" will be seen in—and worked into and be part of— the church!

Let's illustrate it this way.

Here is a young man who has lived with Paul of Tarsus for seven years. He has seen Paul work, fast, pray, start the church, raise it and nurture it. He has lived with the man and experienced the work. He has also eventually seen the church that Paul raised up come under attack. He has seen Paul lied about, spat upon and attacked. He has seen the church almost fall. He has stood wide-eyed at Paul's inverted conduct (always doing the opposite of his natural feelings). This young man has, unconsciously, seen more than he realizes. Being young, having never seen it done "the other way," but always the highest way, he thinks all this suffering, silence, being attacked, being hated, etc., is really easy to handle. He does not yet know the ruthless unprincipled beast that lurks in his own heart.

Finally, one day *he* goes out. He leaves Paul. He is out on the firing line . . . alone. He is a worker.

He is shocked at Christian conduct, dumbfounded at the weakness of the saints, stunned by a close look at the hidden monstrosities of the heart. One day his idealistic roof caves in . . . on him. He is under attack, and he doesn't like it one bit.

One day, for the first time, he gets criticized. Big. Bad. This has never happened to him. He wants to justify himself, to criticize the good-for-nothing heretic who said it. Next, the church he is working with enters into troubled waters. Men doubt his authority, spurn his words, question his leadership. "Problems *Paul* never had," he says. "Or, if he did, I sure never saw them." One day the young man wakes up to find himself in the middle of a full-blown crisis; his back is against the wall. The worst possible thing he feared is about to happen.

He starts thinking. "I've got to get out of this. Let's see, I can do this. Ah, that would stop them." Or, "I can expose this whole thing publicly." Or, "I'll fight; that's what I'll do." "At the next

134

meeting, I'll stand up there and rip them to shreds." "This is too much. That man *has* to be corrected. He has gone too far."

The young worker turns all these possibilities over in his mind. They are all good ideas! Any one will work. And *hundreds* of men have used them. He has a good, sound Scripture for every one of them. In fact, he has only one problem. Only one thing prevents this young man from doing at least one of these guillotinic things. What is that? He can't recall Paul having ever done such a thing!

When he has seen Paul in these same predicaments, he never once saw Paul resort to *this* kind of solution. He racks his brain. Isn't there just once when Paul blew his fuse, read the riot act, or excommunicated someone for this kind of conduct? No, not once.

And at that moment the young man begins to truly realize how disciplined a life Paul lived. How much he guarded his words, and how very, very much Paul had to live in inward agony . . . not allowed, by the cross, to speak. How Paul had to die, daily.

Be sure of this one thing: If this young man *can* find just one single incident in Paul's life when Paul did such-and-such, then he has his justification. *He* will do it, too! Only *he* will do it often, and he will do it with ten times the vendetta he thinks he saw in Paul. Imitating the faults of the one he admires, and doing it with a vengeance.

Mark my words, *you* will scrutinize the worker. You will try to find one flaw. And under pressure, in later years, you will have your excuse, and you will use *his* conduct to justify *your* conduct. You will recall his conduct and you will thereby have your hunting license!

So remember this: Someday you might be a worker! Young saints will be watching *you*. Keep this uttermost before you. And remember, God is more anxious to have a *proper* worker than He is to have the church expressed. Yet the truth is, God *is* more interested in having the church than He is a worker. He is not going to have a proper expression of the church *until* He has proper workers. What do I mean? The worker *precedes* the church; for this reason God must first raise up the worker. You see, your Lord has some terribly high standards for the church. To have those standards a reality, the Lord must require very high standards of the worker. If God starts off with low-grade, compromised workers, He is going to have a disastrous expression of the church.

By the way, your Lord has a way of preventing such disasters. The Lord often prevents the unqualified man from becoming a true *worker.* God stops him short of raising up an expression of church life. You might say God has designed an obstacle course. He puts all the men He calls as workers through this obstacle course.

Look at that obstacle course! Get some idea of how determined God is to have what He wants, how totally He refuses to compromise, and how high—oh how high—is that summit; how unreachable the goal of the standard of the worker.

All right, you start out on this course. You are a young man. You are loose, compromised, terribly sinful, ignorant, and you make a lot of mistakes. But the Lord is liberal . . . especially in the beginning. My point: You can start sloppy, *but* you can't stay that way.

Let me use a perfectly horrible example. Let's say you swear and curse. Now, is that all right? Well, frankly, I don't think so. But the more I see the grace of God in the lives of His children, I have to say it's under the blood and seems to be no hindrance to God's love for you, or His patience to work with you. (The Lord is far more liberal than we humans are.)

So go ahead and swear. But let me ask you a question . . . you who are under grace, and drink . . . you who are under grace, and swear. Answer this question: Do you *really* think God is going to let you continue in that habit and at the same time entrust into your hands the very work of the Kingdom of God?

He will not.

In the life of every worker, God has designed a custom-made obstacle course. Quite a course it is, too! No two courses are alike. One man may find the entire course peppered with one certain obstacle. Another worker may never once face that particular course as long as he lives. He has a *different* set of obstacles altogether. Each man gets a course tailor-made to *his own weaknesses.* What is the purpose of this obstacle course? The answer

136

may sound shocking. But in a very real way that course was designed by God to destroy you . . . *spiritually* destroy you . . . or to expose you, or, at the very least, to *stop* you.

You see, somewhere out past the middle of that course, God begins to entrust the runner with the very work of the Kingdom, God's work on the earth. The course is so designed as to rule out those men unqualified to handle such things. They either fall away or level off at a certain point . . . never to go any higher.

Many men don't know there is such a course. Many certainly don't know they have failed in the running of it.

Let me illustrate. Here is a man called of God. The course is before him. He begins to run. For awhile he runs well. But over and over again, as he comes to crises in his life—to crossroads of suffering, times of indecision—he chooses the more secure route. He doesn't risk the unknown . . . he has a weakness for security. He will not allow his need for security to go to the cross.

Today, where is that man? Selling used cars? No! You will find that man still serving the Lord! He is married to a storybook wife, with two lovely, storybook children, living in a storybook house. He is pastor of a large church, or sits behind a desk in some executive position in his denomination . . . or he's a famous traveling evangelist. By the outward standards, it looks like he ran the course and won. The fact is, he may not have gone past the preliminaries. What if he moved the other direction, the way of suffering, the way of insecurity? God could have taught him much and met him often. He just might have come to know God— in those black hours—in a way few men ever have. Today he might be out accomplishing the very thing closest to the heart of God— entrusted with God's highest dream. (For sure, he won't be sitting behind a desk if this happens!)

There *is* an obstacle course laid down before every worker. If you are such a one then you must run it. If you run it well, some-day (let's say if you start in your early twenties, probably in middle age), He *might* possibly thrust some real work of His Kingdom into *your* hands.

And that is where the obstacle course *really* get rough! Each day is almost unbearable. That is when He *begins* to use the vessel. The test, from then on, is more severe; the boundary between issues more pastel; the lines not clearly drawn; the stakes higher; and the hidden, unknown motives of the heart put on trial more and more.

I look back to my youth. I recall my years in the seminary. The years right after that, when I was still young. I ask: Where are the firebrands, the burning evangels of those days? I was saved in an era of revival. Fiery young men abounded, they boldly preached an extreme Gospel. Now, today! Where are they?

Some have left the ministry; some left the faith. Others shipwrecked. Most sit behind desks. Many got stuck on some early plateau of the Lord's dealings. And don't think the few survivors are safe. Be sure that you are never safe. You see, God doesn't mind shipwrecking workers. They are the lowest common denominator in the Kingdom of God . . . the most expendable. The *last* of all. And always keep in mind that your Lord is more anxious to have a proper worker than He is to have a fully restored church, because He will *not* have the second until He has the first.

You may say that He wants a proper expression of the church more than He wants workers. Of course. Yet the fact remains, the worker comes first. (Adam and Eve. Christ before the church. Ezra before restoration . . . workers before church life.) The church *follows;* so the Lord's *first* interest is in raising up the worker.

But remember this: The Lord has terribly high standards for the church. (It's His *Bride*, you know.) For the church to reach these high standards the Lord must require even higher standards of the worker. If the Lord lets men through who are compromised, then the expression of the church will be a terrible tragedy.

It is for *this* reason (the elimination of workers—the purification of workers), that God designed this obstacle course. "A course is set before me."*

---

* *Please know, dear reader, that I am speaking to people outside of religious organizations. To these people, these truths are far more delineated and observable . . . in their own lives and in the lives of those they cowork with. If you are still in the system, much of what I say may not sound relevant to your situation.*
Remember that I am speaking to a people who are in the practical, daily experience of church life.

I would hardly be fair if I did not venture some guess as to what might await you out there on that course, so I will list a few possibilities:

1. A test of how much you love money.
2. The end of all security.
3. Your moral conduct.
4. Do you lie? Is the truth important?
5. Your willingness to lay down your work and suffer the loss of it all.
6. Will you attack another worker . . . or criticize others?
7. Will you resort to legalism and fear tactics to hold the work together?
8. Can you wait until you are forty . . . or older . . . to begin?
9. Can you submit to another worker?
10. Can you submit to someone else's work . . . one you don't agree with?
11. Will you submit to your peers?
12. Will you split a work, a church . . . for any reason? Will you *allow* others to follow you out of another man's work when you leave it?
13. Will you release your own work . . . leave it forever, giving it into the hands of God?
14. Will you serve a lifetime, without pay, live without money, grow old without a nest egg, do it all with joy and die in poverty, without regret?
15. Will you work and not be lazy?
16. Will you defend yourself when attacked?
17. What will be your definition of a "wolf in our midst," and what will you do with these wolves? (Ditto for "heretics." Christians seem to know it's not nice to attack other Christians, but of course that is not true [!] if the fellow is a wolf or a heretic . . . so most men have a very wide gauge of what a heretic is—very wide indeed. If they could not label men as heretics very easily, they wouldn't be able to attack very many people.)
18. Will you keep growing spiritually when you are old?
19. Will you have "strong convictions about . . . " and will you "stand resolutely against . . . "? Because one of the tricks you will

learn in the Lord's work is (as I make note of later) that you can hold a work together by teaching your people to hate; a unity based on mutual hate of something or someone.

20. Will you give up? Will you fall under the withering fire of constant loss, the endless bombardment of discouragement and failure and setbacks?

21. Will you get angry at God's people? . . . for they are slow to learn and quick to forget.

22. Will you throw around the teaching of "submission" and "authority"? Men who make issues of these teachings prove, in so doing, that they don't have real authority with God.

23. Will you make something other than Christ the centrality of your message, your ministry and your experience?

24. Will all Christians be welcome to share in the fellowship of the Body of Christ regardless of *your* doctrines?

25. Will you be cowardly or courageous under pressure? Uncompromising? (And you ask, "How can I be *meek*—give in, submit, walk away from my work—yet be *courageous?*" Ah, dear brother, that is one thing which makes this course so tough!)

26. Can you live in pain, yet never let it break your spirit?

I could go on. It would take a book to cover the pitfalls, the barriers, the landmines that await you out there. But my point right now is here: May God give you some idea of the impossibility of the course that lies ahead of you . . . may you grasp some idea of how high is the summit the worker is called to scale . . . how unreachable that which you have been called to reach.

Yes, the Lord is gracious . . . and forgiving. Especially at the outset. He can overlook weaknesses—but not forever. Be clear, there are some He will not tolerate, not even at the outset. You can start loose; you can't end that way. And you ought not to ever start that way. You had best begin under discipline. (Not putting *others* under your definition of discipline, but *you* under *God's* discipline. No one else.)

So clean up your life. And crucify the hidden motives of your heart.

Out there at the end of that course—or somewhere out there near the end of it—you pick up the very ministry of Christ. So let's go back to my poor illustration and let's say that you still use curse words way down toward the end of the obstacle course! Oh, it is just a little bit. Listen, there are dear young saints who love the Lord with all their being—they are out there somewhere in the future, perhaps *your* future. There they are, loving the Lord with all their being—and they look up to you with admiration holding you as one higher than an angel. Now you just let fly *one* swear word. Just one. About anything! For any reason! You will either destroy those young hearts, *or* they will imitate your weakness almost as a badge of proof of their utter commitment to you, and of their admiration for you. *And they will outdo you ten fold* in any weakness in your life. Any. And I used swearing as an illustration, but I didn't have swearing in mind. I am speaking of the most minute flaw possible.

Let me put it so bluntly. The Lord *will never* allow you to get through that obstacle course. He will never allow you into such a position as I have just described! A place where the Kingdom depends on you. With such an outrageous flaw? Never! He will move heaven and earth to stop you. You *will be* scrapped! The church is too important in His eyes, the worker too expendable.

I tell you, my impression is that the Lord is willing to sit around in heaven one or two milleniums, waiting to have some men who match His standards, and thereby have His church properly expressed.

Go ahead and enjoy your looseness. You can carry such things for awhile. A cigar here, a pipe there, a can of beer here, a swear word there. All this is far within the permission of grace. But such things are not seen in *any* of those who are still in the running out there in the middle of that course. Those things have either been refined out of a willing runner, or the runner has been set aside, sovereignly, by the Lord.

As I said, this is a poor illustration, but it can serve to make a point clear. Listen as we come to the next message on the worker. Watch as we move to realms so high, standards so rare! You will see how high, how lofty, how unobtainable are the standards of the worker. When we understand the *real* conduct the Lord expects of the worker, these discussions of looseness and sloppiness I used will fall so totally beneath the topic of conversation that they won't even qualify as *poor* illustrations!

(By the same principle, no Christian—be he worker or not—is going on into the deep spiritual realm of the Christian experience still encumbered by these weights. Experience with the Lord and with His cross will have refined those elemental issues out of your life. Either that or the deeper plunge into spiritual experience will have been halted.)

These minor habits I have just used as an illustration totally lose their right to be even listed as issues. On the obstacle course to which I refer those things will have long ago been dropped and forgotten, for that man must have long ago gone on to grapple with truly cataclysmic issues. Do you know what the stakes really are? Do you know the *real* issue under debate? Do you know the *real* outcome that is under question? Do you know the decision that will be settled in this war that is presently being fought??? It is this: The worker is in a battle to decide nothing less than who will rule eternity!

The qualifications you must pass to enter *that* battle are high indeed!

CHAPTER 12

The Loss of the Work

The modern worker: Is he like the ancient workers of the first century? This chapter will answer that question.

Tools. Let's talk once more about tools. Let's talk about the tools that workers today use to make the work work, and the methods workers use to preserve the work. Did the ancient worker use these methods to make the work work and to protect the work?

The first century worker was the most incredible architect in human history. He built the church by the principle that if you lose, you win. Wow!

I hope this chapter shakes you. Deeply. This message challenges the whole premise of the actions of the modern worker when he faces a crisis; that is, when the work of his hand goes into its inevitable crisis. And this is the *inevitable* crisis, the one that must come: *the survival or destruction of his life's work.*

Why pick on this particular premise so much? Because most of the ugly scenes of church history are played out when men are in crises; when their work is threatened. *Then*, yes, truly then, at that time, the real nature of the man surfaces! *Then* the hidden motives of the heart surface. *Then* the ugly side emerges. *Then* the real reason a man is working for God comes out. There *are* hidden motives of the heart. When pressure builds, when your work is under attack, when your work is crumbling, you can spout verses of Scripture all day long to justify what you are doing (that is, to justify your counterattack). But the truth is, the hidden motives of your heart are the things which are provoking you to such action.

What are some of the possible *hidden* motives of the heart? I honestly don't know, but I'd like to guess at a few.

When you see your work about to be destroyed, here are a few hidden—secret—unspoken—unthought *motives of your heart* that may nonetheless be the driving force behind your life. These are the motives you would *never* admit to publicly, but may be the real deciding factor of your conduct.

Unless you do something your work will suffer loss and that means:

(1) You will have no source of income,

(2) you'll lose your place in church history,

(3) you'll be shamed in the community,

(4) you'll lose all your followers and you'll have to start all over again,

(5) a wolf will get *your* flock, and

(6) you will lose any place to minister!

So, to keep your work, you fight back with every tool of the trade. Throughout 1900 years, miserable men have provided this trade with more miserable tools than you can dream exist.

Is that list not accurate? Is it not the real "behind the scenes" reason for so many ugly conflicts between believers??? Listen! I know of no instance in church history where men let their work be destroyed by internal or external opposition (except by sword). Everybody puts up a fight. The fight is usually far worse than the loss would have ever been!

My point is this: I question the justification, that is, I question the *stated* reasons given for *all* the splits in all church history! All of them. I challenge the motives, despite all of the high-sounding reasons given and the scriptural justifications cited.

I go on record as saying that most of the worst head-on collisions between workers come straight out of the black hearts of men. Men protecting their own work when they should let it be ravaged.

All over, in any country today, you see little groups form. (There seem to be zillions of them.) In a few years, someone comes along, joins the group (or was in it at the outset), and there is a disagreement. Then follows a shoot-out or a knock-down drag-out using Bible instead of bullets, Scripture instead of sword.

Let's say that one man starts drawing people away from the group. He either does it by sleight, or by open attack. Bad motives, whatever. The leader sees "his" sheep being led away, and zoom, he hits the roof and starts an open attack on the wolf. Who's at fault? Who knows? All I know are these two things. *First,* what I have just described is the track record of workers for the last 1700 years. On *both* sides of the split. Choose the conduct of either man—neither is justifiable. Both men are without excuse.

The *second:* Dozens, sometimes hundreds, of the Lord's people are damaged beyond repair every time this kind of tragedy takes place between two men. And it happens too often. In fact, somewhere it happens every day. Thousands of God's people are mercilessly destroyed spiritually because of two men and their black, hidden heart motives . . . sailing under the smoke screen of "being scriptural," or something else just as insipid.

I think I can make this clear by illustration.

Let's look at two famous incidents in church history. Luther and Zwingli, Darby and Newton.

Luther and Zwingli

Now the church history books will tell you all about the "great theological controversy that raged" between these first two men. Hogwash. I challenge those men's statements about *why* they split, and I challenge church historians' interpretations. I have watched workers square off ever since I was a child. I've heard their high-sounding reasons, but I have also witnessed their almost savage conduct. No, it is not theology. It is not Scripture. It is men protecting their work . . . at any cost . . . using almost any method . . . looking for any excuse . . . to prevent the loss. We workers have not learned the lesson of losing our lives, and suffering all loss.

145

On to the illustrations.

Luther ignited the Reformation. The time, about 1520. The place, Germany. People and nations all over Europe were leaving the Roman Catholic monolith. They were all "Lutherans." Or at least Luther, and the Germanic states, *wanted* everyone to be Lutherans.

Down in Switzerland there had been raised up yet another figure. Zwingli. When it became evident that Zwingli's influence would prevail in northern Switzerland, and that he was not a Lutheran, then Luther began attacking Zwingli. (He also poked fun at him.) Historians will tell you it was because of doctrinal differences. I sincerely question that premise. First and foremost, it was a heart matter. Luther was threatened. Or better: His work was threatened. When that happens, the man always looks (1) at the other man's teachings and (2) at his life. He *will* find fault with the other man's teachings . . . and the other man's life. There is no question about it. He *will* find fault. Even if he has to invent a counter theology to the other man's teaching, right out of thin air. Instant theology! Needed to smokescreen the black motives of the heart. I strongly suspect the heart. More specifically, the threatened work is the motivation, the fountainhead, of *most* of the new theology that was invented during the Reformation (the period that saw more new theology invented than any other) and all ages since then. Let me put it simply: The hidden motive of the heart is the mother of most new theology and most theological battles.

Anyway, the attacks on Zwingli became more vicious. Friends on both sides tried to get them together. Maybe peace—and even union—could come from it. So finally, in 1529 the two men met in the city of Marburg, Germany. They agreed on thirteen of the fourteen points under consideration. On the fourteenth they agreed on half. It was thirteen and one half, to one half.

I quote one writer's record:

"Luther himself says that Zwingli begged with tears in his eyes . . . saying, 'There are no people on earth with whom I would rather be in harmony than with the Wittenbergers.' He would not, however, surrender his position that the Lord's Supper . . . was simply the grateful remembrance of it by faithful souls . . . .On that point Luther was adamant – 'impudent and obstinate' – and, in the end [Luther] brushed his Swiss brethren off. 'You have a different spirit from ours,' Luther said."

From this story you will probably side with Zwingli. I don't blame you. Gentle. More tolerant. Less doctrinal, obviously. (Don't be too quickly taken in. This is not the end of the story.)

The two groups, nonetheless, never joined. In fact, I believe Zwingli's unwillingness to jump into Luther's camp may be the reason Luther found so much righteous indignation and shock in Zwingli's terrible doctrine.

Zwingli made one mistake. He—and *his* followers—just wanted to *fellowship* with the Lutherans. I believe there would have been a different story if they had come to *join* the Lutheran movement. If they had come to join, Luther would not—I believe— have been threatened. The story would have been totally different.

Despite Zwingli's noble efforts, Luther wasn't about to yield any geography. He protected his work, his territory: northern Europe. Zwingli was an external threat to Luther. Luther wanted only Lutherans on the earth. Zwingli was a territorial threat.

But Zwingli had territory, too. And he had a work. And there was an internal threat to *Zwingli's* work in Zurich. Let's see just how noble a fellow he is back home.

Every urban county (canton) in northern Switzerland had joined Zwingli's reformation. But back home Zwingli was "Luther," and he had some little "Zwinglis" giving him a fit. Was he more gracious to those threatening *his* work?

Zwingli's threat was a group called the Swiss Brethren. The Swiss Brethren are the ones who should have taken the Reformation. And they would have, except for one thing—the sword. More of these "radicals" were put to death in religious persecution than all the other groups combined. The radicals in every country were virtually blotted out. Tens of thousands, possibly millions. Today, it is called genocide.

Here is the record of what happened just to the leaders of the Swiss Brethren. *Grebel* was banished and died of the plague; *Mantz* was drowned—by Zwingli's city council—in Lake Zurich; *Blaurock* was flogged and banished under penalty of death; *Hubmeier* was burned at the stake in Vienna.

How did all this happen? You might know, Zwingli started it. He was threatened by this little band; therefore he did what Luther did. In fact, in the same year Luther rejected Zwingli, Zwingli rejected the Brethren. Of course, being a man more gentle than Luther, you expect him to be more gracious than Luther was to him! (Well, never underestimate what a worker will do when his work is threatened.)

Read here the decree the city council of Zurich put into law. The council did this under the direct influence of Zwingli.

We are determined not to tolerate the re-baptized within our borders. There must be no fellowship with them whatever.

Later, in the Imperial Edict of 1529, they decreed

that every re-baptized person, of whatever age or sex, be put to death by sword, or fire, or otherwise. All preachers – and those who help them – all who persist, or relapse, must be put to death. There will be no pardon.

The blood bath that followed, reaching all the way from the Atlantic to the eastern frontiers of Europe, is one of the most hideous, unbelievable chapters in the annals of mankind.

And now I will come to the end of the story. I have just told you (1) what Luther, a Protestant, did to a Protestant, and (2) what another Protestant—Zwingli—did to the Brethren. Now let's be ecumenical and record what the Catholics did.

Yes, two years later the Catholics got into the act. The rural cantons of northern Switzerland got together an army and marched on Zwingli's Zurich.

Zwingli's Protestant army met the Catholic army. Zwingli's side lost. The Catholic soldiers searched the battlefield for Zwingli's body until they found it. They built a dunghill, put Zwingli's body—along with a pig's—on it, chopped up the pig, chopped up Zwingli and burned the remains together on the dunghill.

You may think this a terrible story. The worst in church history. No. It is a typical story! And the whole story you've just read covers only three years! This is a story the likes of which you can find on almost any page of church history from about 350 to 1700. Three not too remarkable years!

That is Christianity. *That* is the religious system. But most of

all, *that* is the way of religious man, the servant of God, mind you
—the worker—when his territory is threatened! Let a worker feel
his work is in jeopardy, and you have a man capable of doing
almost anything! And he will give you a good, sound, scriptural
reason for it when he is through. Luther did. Zwingli did. The
Catholics did.

And that attitude still lives today. And that attitude, and that
kind of conduct, must end with us. This is our mission.

More of the Same

In the last illustration, we talked about three "in-the-religious-
system" groups (Luther, Zwingli and the Catholics) and one "out-
of-the-religious-system" group (the Swiss Brethren).

By the way, there is an interesting case here of history
repeating itself . . . or at least a good illustration of fallen man's
sectarian nature.

The Swiss Brethren didn't persecute. They were persecuted.
But listen to this: The only real survivors of the Swiss Brethren are
the Mennonites. The Mennonites suffered so much (rivalling
almost anyone in church history) for a century or more. You would
think these people—pacifists if you please—would never, ever
stoop to do what their enemies did. But, along about 1750 a
Mennonite wrote a book that was a vicious attack on the Moravian
brethren. That book was untrue, but it was believed, and it dogged
the Moravian brethren for a century, breeding all sorts of unbelievable—but believed—stories about them. And so the sad story
goes.

Well, you haven't heard enough sad stories, so let me tell you
another.

From 325 to 1520, Romanism had the corner on persecution.
After that, from 1520 until about 1750, all the state churches—that
is, all the large, tax-sponsored denominations—got into the act of
killing, burning, drowning, hanging and quartering their fellow

Christians. It was the folks on the bottom of this totem pole, the radical groups (usually with the word "brethren" in their nickname), who caught most of the persecution. They persecuted no one. *Folks outside the religious system persecuted no one.* Not in those days. They were the persecutee, not the persecutor.

Oh, they denounced the religious system. Did they ever. But the Christians in the *third* stream *never* persecuted either the Protestants or the Catholics.

Then along came religious liberty. The age after 1750. You, an individual, or you, a group, could now step out of structured Christianity without getting imprisoned or killed for it. Would you believe, a short time later a totally new development sprung up in church history. Behold, believers *outside* the system began attacking one another! In fact, they grasped the same scandalous tool the religious world had wielded for a thousand years—attacking one another because the other guy didn't "believe right."

And here is my second sad story. It is not a well known story, but it had great influence on the faith. It is the story of what men *outside* the religious system did.

Darby and Newton

It is about 1820. The place is Dublin, Ireland. One of the greatest twenty-year periods in church history is about to begin.

A group of Christians began meeting in Dublin. Their emphasis was on a simple meeting with no clergy present.

The meetings were electric. The movement began to grow. A little later there was, I believe, a shift in the emphasis. Rather than magnetic *meetings* that had Christ as Head, a shift was made toward a strong Biblical teaching ministry. (A "me talk, you listen" kind of meeting grew up. The whole freeness and openness that marked the earlier meetings began to decline somewhat.) Why the change?

This shift was brought on by a man who has probably influenced church history as much as any one single man with the exception of Luther. You may have never heard of him. His name is John Darby. He is the father of present-day evangelical, fundamental Christianity. He single-handedly, out of thin air, invented today's most popular view of premillenialism, and, in a way, invented that whole doctrine. He is the father of eighty percent of all the fundamental and evangelical doctrines men teach today. His teachings are so widely held, so accepted to be the proper interpretation of Scripture, that most people don't even know they have learned a doctrinal system at all. Darbyism *is* the Scripture to most evangelicals.

Well, Darby, shortly after joining the Brethren movement, dominated it. Soon it was a Bible teaching movement. There were about two dozen great teachers in it. The magnetism of the "headless" meeting soon faded. Most of the people just sat, sang and listened. (Except at the Lord's Supper meeting. There were no speakers there, so the believers got to share. Those meetings were glorious, we are told.) By the way, the teachers were among the greatest teachers in church history. They have virtually no peers. What those lay-people listened to as they sat out there on those chairs was some of the greatest stuff since the Apostles.

Now comes the sad part.

A really large work grew up in the city of Plymouth, England. Darby was the central figure in that group.

Darby decided to travel. He left, and he was gone for years. While he was away, a man named Newton emerged as the leader at Plymouth. The people followed *Newton.*

Shortly after Darby got back home, he accused Newton of heresy. Just like that. Bang. Rank, non-Christian, flagrant, ungodly, dangerous heresy.

Newton repented, all over the place. The Newton repentance was "not adequate enough." Darby said that everyone who even heard Newton and agreed with him was now contaminated, and no one was to have fellowship with that person. Darby told all the other assemblies that they could not accept anyone from Plymouth in their meetings, unless they renounced Newton. If any assembly in another city should happen to accept these people, then that whole assembly was also excommunicated from the movement. It, too, by fellowshipping with even *one* who had fellowshipped with Newton, was contaminated.

Now, *there* is a neat cure for stopping a threat to your work! *There* is quite a way to keep a threat from spreading. In fact, Darby invented a brand new scriptural doctrine—right out of thin air—to fit the occasion and solve the problem of his threatened work: He *proved* from Scripture that these people were unclean, and that in Apostolic days churches treated "unclean" Christians this very same way.

And, furthermore, the people believed Darby.

Well, over 120 years have now passed. Some of the Brethren are still fighting over that incident like it happened last Tuesday. The "open" Brethren tell you "Version No. 1," the "closed" Brethren will tell you "Version No. 2." Both look at it as a great doctrinal matter.

I would not be too far from the truth if I said that—even today —some of them are more apt to fellowship with an animistic Zulu than they are with one another!

I'd like to tell you my own feelings about the whole thing. I question everything told in the whole incident . . . especially the part about "being true to the faith once delivered." Heresy was not the issue. A new scriptural doctrine was not the issue— *doctrine* was not the issue. "Defending the faith" was not the issue. The *work* was the issue. Darby was threatened. The rest was an invention (a smoke screen). Maybe not even thought in the mind, but in the heart . . . it was simply a matter of a threatened work.

The work was threatened. Someone picked up a tool, accusing a man of near-fiendish heresy, accusing a man of being unfaithful to the Scripture . . . and used it to regain control of the movement.

Don't look down on the Plymouth Brethren. This is only *one* illustration. There is another like it on every page of church history. And in *every* case they fight with one another like it was the first—and only—dispute in history, and that the throne itself was at stake.

We always fight when our work is threatened. Always. And we get vicious. Every page of church history is witness to that fact. Read the history of any denomination. Go to any "Jesus house," go into any home Bible class, visit any "free group" or "home meeting," go to any interdenominational organization headquarters. Ask. You will get the same story.

Workers fight. Workers accuse. Workers invent "instant doctrinal heresy" with which to chop up their opponent. Workers split. Workers split churches and movements. Workers write pamphlets, workers denounce one another—and I will go even further: If given the lawful right to do so by the state, workers even kill one another!

And now we come to our point.

Needed: A New Breed of Workers

There must be born on this earth a new breed of workers. Men who do not attack, criticize, condemn, or more succinctly: men who do not protect their work. Men who will stand right there and let their life's work be destroyed. They will let men wreck their work, but come what may they are resolved *they will not fight.*

I know. You may say, "That is not scriptural." You may be right. Then I will answer that the situation today, and in the past, is so appalling that it is time for a higher position than that which men today repair to as the "scriptural" way.

This is not unprecedented. Paul once observed: "The scriptural way for a worker to receive his income is by having it given to him by the church where he ministers. 'A laborer is worthy of his hire. You don't muzzle the ox when it is grinding wheat.' But for me . . . I PAUL, TAKE A WAY HIGHER THAN THE WAY PRESCRIBED. I *work* for a living! I refuse to be paid. I go higher than the prescribed standard."

I am aware that the present (and past) interpretation of Scripture is to defend your work at all cost. "Be a defender of the faith." I've read the verse that says, "therefore, be on the alert for wolves." With that, men axe up anything within three counties that fits *their* interpretation of a "wolf." Men have murdered with that verse; and to this hour, that verse is used to justify some of the most horrible conduct imaginable.

I challenge this interpretation. First, there is nothing of the cross in it. No suffering. No loss. *God's* work is always built on loss. Next, such a view does not match the example of Jesus Christ. Lastly, I challenge the notion that Paul *ever* did such a thing. I'm saying that Paul never attacked those "wolves" he spoke of!!!

A quick overview will not do. I can't "prove" this with a verse of Scripture. We will have to reconstruct the historical setting of all his letters, of his whole life (not using scissored verses taken out of context and historical background), and see what Paul was talking about. When we do, a totally different Paul just might emerge. And all those verses may have a totally different ring.

Beware the individual verse.

And *now* I will quote a verse!

Paul made a most interesting remark about dissension, about conflict. He said, "These things need be." He took the opposite view. Not "Save the work" . . . "Prevent the clash" . . . "Throw the rascal out" . . . or "These things should *not* be." Or more to the point, "In order to ensure unity in our movement, we are now passing the following 387 rules. Obey them or you are a rebel."

"These things *need* be." Paul said *that!*

Why? "Paul, why are church crises needed?"

So that it might be shown who is approved.

There are wolves. There always have been, there always will be. Don't try to stop them. *These things need be* . . . that it might be shown who is approved.

"But the flock will be scattered! Many will be hurt. No! We must shepherd the flock. Paul did." Oh! Did he? If he did, was it with the same spirit you have? And besides, are you Paul? By what right do you claim the position of Paul in church history? There

154

may be legitimate grounds for so doing. But those legitimate grounds are found in suffering, bearing the cross, in meekness and brokenness. Not in axe handles!

Well, let's talk about that. Please tell me about the night an angel came down to your room, tapped you on the shoulder and said, "Go start a church." (Or was it an interdenominational, non-profit, tax-exempt mission to blue-eyed, left-handed albinos in the north-east corner of town?) Just because you got a group of people meeting together, is that suddenly *God's* work? *You* started that work. What right do you have of quoting all those verses and applying them to an *organization* that you and you alone started? Whence did you become submiss*or* and they submiss*ee?* How did *you* earn the place of authority? Which angel in heaven gave it to you? By what magic did this come about?

I question that Paul *ever* chopped up a wolf. "These things need be." By what right do you chop up wolves—and what makes your group a "flock" anyway???

What right do you have to suddenly grab the sacred Scripture and start quoting all those verses as though they applied to *your* work?

"Guard the flock over which *God* made *you* overseer?" Who, besides you, said you are an overseer? Because a man has the ability to put a hundred people together to meet doesn't justify him in saying, "This applies to us." Did *God* make you overseer, or did *you* make you overseer?

Who sent you? Were you sent? By God? I doubt it. I seriously doubt it. Not by the evidence of your conduct toward your "wolves."

But there is one way to know. There is a way, it appears, to know if you have been approved by God, and that *yours* is a flock!

"These things must be that we may know who is approved."

Are *you* approved? Does chopping up wolves prove that you are approved? Or does it prove the very opposite?

Let me illustrate: A man starts a work (his work). It meets for two years. A split starts to develop. This *will* happen. It will happen every time. To this fact there has virtually never been an exception. There probably never will be. Every work goes through a crisis. And when the crisis comes, watch! The verses come out. The axe comes out. The "doctrinal differences" appear out of thin air.

The whole basis the leader operates from—his whole theory as he quotes verses, as he attacks, writes articles, accuses—is this: The work must be preserved, the flock must be protected, people must be protected from harm (i.e., from the local competition). This is the thesis—the theorem—of the worker: "My work *must* be preserved." There is no other consideration. But the opposite may just be true, my brother. It may be that in this crisis your Lord is testing you. The highest thing may not be to preserve, but to totally, utterly, lose! To do otherwise is to prove you are unapproved.

All your fussing, accusing, attacking, is to preserve *your* work. Selfish, self-centered, frightened, *self*-crowned . . . fear stricken child.

All your effort to preserve *your* work is proof God didn't send you. And it's proof that the work is your work, not God's work. And you are frightened. You are afraid that unless you fire every cannon and employ every tool, your newly-founded work will collapse; collapse because some evil monster is in your midst. You are afraid. Scared. Yet you speak of "authority" and "submission," and your words are tough, bold and harsh. But God is not with you. Your efforts at preservation are proof He is not with you. "These crises need to come." Crises are not to be nipped, fought, suppressed. They are to be accepted, embraced . . . without a murmuring word . . . not a hand of resistance. These things are needed so we can tell, so God can tell, so the angels can tell which men are approved!

If God had sent you—truly sent you—you would not do these things to the men who threatened your work. God's work is *God's* work. *What God has done cannot be destroyed.* I repeat: God's work cannot be destroyed. What *you* do is going to fall apart—someday—no matter how much you jump up and down.

Catholics should not have murdered the brethren in the dark ages. If those Catholics had been God's work, then those little free groups could not have hurt them! Luther, Zwingli, et al: for

156

shame. Your volcanic eruptions were proof of your own fears, your own lack of confidence that God was with you. If you are God's work, that work will survive a crisis. Sure, there will be loss—yes, your loss (yes, numerical loss), but not God's loss. What God has done can't be lost. Pray tell, what is your excuse for protecting your work? What is your excuse for such reprehensible, vicious, ungodly attacks on your very own brother?

I dare you. I double dare you to walk away from your work right at the worst time. Do you have the courage? Are you that sure of your ministry? Do you believe that what you said will stand? Are you confident enough in your message, of your followers, of the peace of God in you? And most of all, are you so certain God sent you for this task that you can walk away from it . . . knowing it doesn't matter? I doubt you have the courage. And *that* is proof your conduct (your attacks on others) is *wrong*. Sent men are not afraid, and they don't protect. They know . . . *these crises need be!!!*

Most men who head up a work live in fear: fear that if the work they head up should fall apart, they will never be able to put together another one. Here is something men say in their hearts at the time their work is under attack (but which they would never say out loud because it reveals the true intent and motive of the heart): "This is my only chance to have a work, to prove God is with me. If I fail here, *this* may be the end. So I'd better bow my back, and start throwing out the men who are causing my problem." Fear. Fear of losing one's big chance. Fear of disgrace. Fear of loss of reputation. Fear of failure. FEAR. Because God has not sent you!

And what will happen to these precious works so thoroughly protected by such bloody means? What happens to men who go through crises, fighting all the way? What happens to them? After the fight is over, what is left? Sometimes a work survives . . . barely . . . but only by the bloodiest means. And for years afterward the survivors go on speaking about and damning the others involved. This is *not* the proper conduct of a man of God no matter what has been done to him.

And the other side. (There are two sides.) What happened to all the people that got called "heretics"? What happens to these people who got thrown out of the group? What happens to so many of the leaders—in both factions—especially if the movement is badly damaged and there is a great deal of numerical loss? What usually happens to men left totally without followers? When the whole mess is over, they become disappointed and bitter. Do they shake off the tragedy??? Do they continue to love Him? Do they continue in that vision they preached? Do they go back, without rancor or bitterness—but rather with *joy*—to build again? You know the answer to this! No, they do not! *This* is proof, *again,* that they were not sent. Proof, *again,* that it was man's work, not *God's* work. Yes, *these* things need be. *Here* is part of the obstacle course you must run! And a crisis is put in your life—by God Himself—so that all the universe can see *your conduct.* Answer for yourself, were you approved, or disqualified?*

It is good, necessary and terribly important (and it is also an absolute certainty) that your work *will be* tried by *fire!!!* Hope for that day. Expect that day. And when it comes, get out of the way and let the fire fall. Whatever is left, whatever remains which is untarnished, unmelted, undamaged—*that is the work of God.*

Perhaps now you can grasp the depth of what I mean when I say there must be a new breed of workers on this earth: men who will not fight; yes, men who can build what fire can't destroy. Men who, after the crisis is over, are found approved, truly, truly, overtly approved by God. Men who are not afraid. Men who can see, and are willing to see, their whole work destroyed. In other words, *sent* men. Fearless men, fearless—not because they are mean—but fearless because they know they are not important, nor is their work; and they fear *God* because they only want *God's* work (not *their* work) on this earth.

"These things need be that we may *know* who is approved!" It is a two-fold *knowing:* The worker is approved because his work

---

Consider two used car lots, across the street from one another. Customers are limited! Listen to the stories each salesman tells his customers about the man across the street. "He's a crook." "He sells stolen cars." "The F.B.I. is investigating him." "He's being sued by Eskimos." Now you and I understand that kind of talk. But we often fail to realize it is exactly the same circumstances and the same motives that cause a man to call another group in town "heretical" and "cultist" and "of the devil." The conflicts of church history are so often just used car salesmen battling it out with a theological vocabulary.

survived the fire (alone and unaided by him). And we can be fairly sure that the *believers* who came out on the other side unscorched are *also* approved because *they* too survived the fire. I see only *gain* in such a work! God, give us men who will not fight, but men who will lose—*all,* if necessary.

To see such men raised up: This is our mission.

CHAPTER 13

The Conduct of a Worker: An Example

We are talking about workers. In the next few messages I would like to talk to you about Paul. I would like to tell you a little bit about the unknown Paul.

First of all, I would like for you to see how limited God made Paul when a crisis arose; how boxed in God had him; how little the Lord allowed him to do in a crisis. He was so boxed in, so limited, that sometimes, during times of crisis, he did so little that he looked ridiculous.

This is the way it must be. The Lord's servant is given so *few* things he can do to protect the work; so few—if any—ways to defend himself or even to survive. The worker is pushed into a corner. He can say nothing, do nothing. He looks like he doesn't even have the mental capacity to marshal a good defense, or come up with the simplest solution. Consequently, he *looks* like he *has* no defense . . . therefore it appears his opposition is right and he is wrong. After all, if he were right he could say *something!* Before the world, before his pursuers and destroyers, he emerges in a crisis not as the strong man of God, but instead, the village idiot. Sink he will. Lose he will. There is no hope. A child could win against him.

Now how can a true servant of God get himself into such a mess? And this is what we shall see: It is *God* who put him into such a helpless situation. How? A good question. Let us see the answer.

God calls you. At the outset of your life the Lord lets you get away with so much. You make mistakes. He looks the other way. But ten years later? You are so limited, so boxed in. You have almost no tools you can turn to that will aid your survival. He has disarmed you against attack. This is a mark of the servant of God. Boxed in!

A worker in a crisis is a disarmed, boxed in man. He is not that fearless, shoot-from-the-hip, western gunslinger-type who rides into town and stares down the villain. Rather, the worker in a crisis is, or should be, an unarmed, defenseless man. Rather than the national hero, he often looks more like the town dunce. In crises, God boxes in His servants, leaving them nothing to do, except suffer . . . and lose.

Will you ever arrive at a point where, spiritually, you have become so truly, honestly helpless? Yes. But not by your efforts. And don't suppose you can fake so high a walk. You *can't.* Not this. You see, to come to a place where you never rise in your own defense is a lifetime project of transformation. And you can be sure that God alone is in charge of this project.

Let's turn to Paul's life; then you will understand what I am saying. Let's try to get to know this man. In so doing we will see the high standard of the worker . . . in a crisis.

First, please look at his letters. He wrote thirteen in all. From these letters we learn the man. Let's look at the nature of his letters.

Three Introductory Letters

Romans, Colossians and the circuit letter, Ephesians, are letters to people Paul had never met. Because these are letters to new churches he had never seen, they give us an idea of his spoken ministry. Romans, Colossians and Ephesians . . . the content of these letters is what he *would have said* if he had been there in person! In other words, what is written to these three churches is probably what men *heard* in the rest of the churches. None of the other letters tell us what Paul spoke to young churches. We do not get an extensive idea of the content of Paul's message from those other letters. These three letters and a few lines in Acts are our best hint.

Two Very Personal Letters

In Philippians and Philemon, you catch the man as you would know him if he were your personal friend. These are very intimate letters: one to a beloved church, one to a personal friend.

Three Letters to Young Apostles

These are two letters to Timothy and one to Titus.

The Five Crisis Letters

That leaves five letters. And it is from these five letters that Paul gets his "tough guy" image. From these letters men justify their ugly attacks and their grounds to be "defenders of the faith."

These five letters are the crisis letters. All five were written to churches, and all the churches involved were in crises at the time he wrote. All these churches were established churches, churches he had *left*.

One letter was written to the four churches of Galatia. Paul was hopping mad when he wrote it. This was probably his first letter, written about 51 A.D., just after his first journey.

Two of the letters were to the church in Thessalonica (written on his second journey). The church was about one year old.

The last two of these five "crisis" letters were written to the church in Corinth, about six years after the birth of the church there. When he wrote these two letters he was facing almost certain death and was living in the worst, darkest moments he had ever experienced in his life.

Let's take a fresh look at those "crisis" letters. In all of these five letters he tells us different things about himself no one ever knew before. We just might get a new view of Paul, and we may get some idea of God's work and His high standards for a worker, especially a worker in the middle of a crisis. And, methinks, you might have to give up your "tough guy" image of Paul.

What about the Galatian letter? It was written to the four churches that were raised up on Paul's first journey, probably about a year after he left them.

Two crisis letters are the Thessalonian letters, written in the middle of his second journey. The church addressed is one year old.

The last two crisis letters are the Corinthian letters. The second is especially a crisis letter, for Paul was hiding his predicament when he wrote the *first* letter. You have to read the second letter to see what a horrible, pitiful mess he was in when he wrote the first one!

All right, let's look at this man. And may you discover things you never dreamed of and catch a glimpse of the high standard of conduct set by this worker. A standard that is lost in our age. A standard that must be regained. Come with me on an imaginary journey with Paul.

Entering a New City

Let's imagine Paul is about to enter a city for the first time. As he enters, he hopes to see the church raised up in that city. Think of all the things he knows! (Imagine cities like Thessalonica and Corinth.) For instance, he knows he is despised: despised in the last town, despised in the town before, despised in Damascus, hated in Jerusalem. He knows he will speak in the local synagogue. And he knows that in a few days, or a few weeks at best, he is going to be thrown out of that building, *never* to be allowed back in again.

164

He knows that later on this whole town will turn against him and probably try to kill him, or at least drive him out of the city and banish him from the territory. He knows the church will be left all alone, and he knows—brother, you had better be certain—he *emphatically, assuredly knows* exactly what dangers and what evils await the church out there in the future.

Paul knows every bit of this—knows everything that is going to happen to that assembly of believers that doesn't even exist yet! On the very day he arrives, he knows! He knows it *all*.

The circumcision party will arise. The false brethren (the workers with their Judean gospel), the fakes, the money-motivated men; the dissension, divisiveness, the whole rotten, stinking mess. He knows it all. I repeat: *He knows.*

Yet, in all the time he stays in that city he will *never* speak of those things. He will do nothing to warn or prepare those dear, innocent people of the quagmire they are about to be dragged through. There was so much he knew, and it is incredible how little he spoke of the mess which would follow.

What did he talk about? Well, what would you have talked about? What do workers today talk about? They talk about, preach about the topics which I have just listed, of course. Workers spend a large part of their ministry just warning the Lord's people of dangers! Paul spoke of none of those things. It was as though he didn't know them—even though he had just been through about all of them in the town he just left.

What did he talk about? He talked about Christ. He won the lost. He ministered Christ. That's all they got out of him: Christ.

Yes, Paul had a lot stored away in his heart. For instance, he knew he was called of God. He knew he had been sent by God. Most of all, he knew *why* he had been sent. That was the hardest part. He knew so much depended on him. Beyond that, Paul had revelation of Christ; revelation so great it was unlawful to speak of it. But he knew some negative things, too. As I've already said, he knew men would come and try to lead away each church he raised up. The most dangerous thing was this: *Paul knew how to stop those men!* He knew the dangers each church faced. He could prepare them for these dangers. He could sit down with them and tell them all the sordid details of the whole sorry mess that had come before. He could tell them what kind of people would be coming to the city and what they would be saying and doing. He could present these "false brethren" in the worst light, belittle them and attack them. He *could* stop those men. He *could* protect those churches. He could guarantee their survival. He could secure an impregnable defense against all the coming enemies. But Paul was a wise man. There was something else he knew: He knew if he did all those things he would rip out the very heart and soul of the church. He would have succeeded in saving those little assemblies, but he would have brought into existence on this earth something less than Christ and something less than the church of Jesus Christ.

Let's go on. What are some of the things Paul knew? He knew one day he would have to leave this city. He would have to say goodbye to saints. He knew they would be young. He knew they would be fragile. Most of all, thank God, he knew they would be *innocent.* He knew that he would suffer to raise up this church. Sometimes out there he would cry all night, or pray all night. Some nights he would have to do both. He would fast. He would be asked a thousand elementary questions, go through hundreds of crises with individual brothers and sisters. He would pour out his life blood. He would work eight to ten hours a day in the hot sun; never receive one cent from the church. Sometimes he would be thanked. Sometimes he would probably be criticized for not having done more.

He would toil. He would sweat. He would risk his life. One day he would probably bleed; possibly be stoned. He would work harder for those people, give more of his life than any man on earth would have given; pour out more for them and more on them than any other man would ever dream of doing. He had every right to those churches and he had every right to feel protective.

But there was something more he knew. He knew how important these eight or ten little churches were. Small, scrubby, dinky, gentile to the core. Rough. Loose. All of that. Yes, it was true. Unimportant looking. Yet Paul knew something about these churches: He knew they were the purest expression of the church on the whole earth. He knew the gospel he preached was the purest gospel on this whole planet. In fact, he knew that the whole future course of the Kingdom of God on this earth depended on the success of this little handful of scrubby churches. Everything, the whole destiny of eternity, hung on these dinky people.

Why? Because he knew that a true, pure, liberated gospel had raised up these churches, and *only* in *these* churches was the purity of the gospel preserved. His gospel was a better gospel than that which was being experienced in Judea. And the expression of the church was a higher expression than that which was known among the Jewish believers. In other words, Paul knew the destiny of salvation, of Christ's ministry, of the gospel, of the Kingdom, of all future Christian history, rested with these people. He knew this to be a fact. In fact, this was his "sending." Paul knew this and he lived with this frightening knowledge *every* day.

As I said, he knew that out there somewhere were men coming to destroy these churches, to destroy God's work on the earth. So it was high time for him to go into the protecting business! If ever in all the course of human events a man needed to preserve and protect, that time was *now*. Paul knew this. He had better get into the business of warning, listing all the frightening possibilities of the future, instructing the saints, showing them exactly how to recognize the imminent dangers, how to be cautious of outsiders, leery of other teachings and all sorts of wolves out there ready to devour an innocent people. Paul had surely better do a good job of warning them of heinous people, and of foreboding pitfalls.

And for sure, that's exactly what we think he did! I believe you have the distinct impression that he told each church, "Those dirty unmentionables are going to come here. They're going to tell you about circumcision. They're going to attack me. Beware. Don't listen. They follow me wherever I go, trouble me, persecute me, lie about me, stone me. They may arrive any day after I leave. Don't listen to these terrible people."

That is our image of Paul. And this is also the way workers have been talking and acting for hundreds of years. And they so often justify their conduct on the basis of Paul. But if we workers would stop and look at our black hearts, we would know our motives are not high and holy, but they are born rather out of fear, greed and ambition. It is not allegiance to the Scripture and it is not high and honorable motives that direct us, but rather it is the darkest parts of humanity that cause a man to protect his work. It has been the unbroken custom of the ages for workers to warn (or is it *over*warn?) Christians against enemies, heretics, "demonic doctrines," devilish teachings, etc., etc., etc. The tragedy is, such talk is so often aimed at a man who was once a former friend. Something is amiss here somewhere!

We warn the Lord's people against bad doctrine. "Don't believe in once saved, always saved: it's of the devil." "Don't believe in anything except once saved, always saved: everything else is of the devil." We warn against men. Sometimes we do this blatantly, sometimes we do it even more powerfully than that: We do it with the subtlety of a raised eyebrow. We are masters of psychology. Someone called it the ability to damn a man by means of faint praise.

My brother, just try giving dear simple Christians a steady diet of all these foreboding possibilities. Warnings, warnings and more warnings. Just look around you. See what it does to their childlike innocence. See what it does to their inherent purity. See what it does to their openness. See what it does to brotherly love. God help us, brothers. This conduct has got to go.

Back to Paul.

Thank God, there was one more thing Paul knew . . . or that God taught him: He knew you cannot build the church on negatives. You cannot build the church by discussing the sordid past, or by warning men about a dangerous future. Paul could have built a church on "Beware of the Circumcision," "Beware of the Jews," "Beware of 10,000 things." He could have built a church this way. I'm afraid many men do. But what would the people be like? Why, they would be people spending all their time turning over every rock, looking under every tree, staring down every hole, trying to find just one of those cussed circumcisers so they could bean him good with a sandal. They would have spent all their time warning the Lord's people, bringing up the negatives; this is exactly what the Lord's people will do when they are fed a steady diet of warnings!

But surely Paul did take some precautionary measures against all these dangers? After all, if he did not warn the Lord's people in some way, they would all end up being circumcised and everything would be lost. What did he do?

He did absolutely nothing.

Paul was a man limited by God. He was boxed in.

Look at us today. We stand in the midst of all sorts of very real dangers. (And we also stand in the midst of an awful lot of imaginary ones.) Christians in our age grow up on men's teachings, men's doctrines; they are told that *these* doctrines are for their benefit! "The Bible says that you are commanded to know all these doctrines." But many of these doctrines (and if the truth were known, probably *most* of these doctrines) were invented out of thin air ages ago, instant and on the spot, by men trying to protect their work! We are told we need to be warned against this, protected against that, to have nothing to do with "them" and that "he" is a rank heretic. The church must be protected, warned, and guarded against so many, many evils. Rot! Garbage! Hogwash! Such warnings don't help Christians. They destroy Christians, unbalance them, steal their innocence, make them sectarian. And worse, innocent Christians suddenly turn into inspectors and protectors. Negativism is born. It makes them so legalistic and protective, so narrow-minded their ears touch. Simple, dear, pure, beautiful, loving, uncomplicated Christians lose their openness to *all* saints. Most of all, our super-overprotection fills them with fear: fear of shadows, fear of things that don't exist. Innocence and purity are lost for the sake of preserving a work. Tragedy of tragedies. I repeat: A work that needs to be preserved isn't worth preserving. Or, to put it another way, we end up with less than Christ. A lot less.

I can almost hear someone back there on the back row saying, "Gene, you lose the case. Look at the letter to the Galatians. Paul ripped into those people unmercifully, warning them about all sorts of dangers." You're absolutely correct, but please stop looking at the Scripture as if it was a compilation of individual proof texts. (We've had enough of that, too.) This letter was written by a living, breathing man to a living, breathing people, and they were in a very special situation. This book, like every book in the New Testament, has a historical setting.

Paul was snarling when he wrote Galatians. Yes, he was swinging right and left. But this is proof of the real heart of God that was in Paul. First, these churches, remember, were raised up on the first journey. Second, Paul, with Barnabas, had come into each of those four cities presenting Christ and nothing but Christ. The church was raised up. No warnings, no protection. Paul and Barnabas left. The people they left were lambs surrounded by wolves. They had *no* warnings of dangers. They were reveling in their purity, innocence and freedom. Yet Paul probably suspected what would happen to these churches. He also knew how much he had suffered for them. And yet, despite all that, he did not warn them. It was only *after* (please notice the word "after") the party of the circumcised had come through Galatia that he finally spoke out so clearly on the issue. It was not until after his work was in the fire and the churches knew they were in a crisis that he began to speak *on things he had known for years.* If you doubt this, just look at Galatians and II Corinthians a little more closely. In both places, the record is so clear! Those Christians, in both towns, received Paul's enemies with open arms! The Christians in Galatia and Corinth took these "false brethren" in, fed them, believed them and almost followed them. Some almost to the point of renouncing Paul and his gospel. You don't do things like that unless you happen to be totally innocent and totally unwarned!

No! Paul did *not* attack his avowed enemies. He never even mentioned their existence!!!

But would all of you workers out there please notice something? Paul's work *stood* in the hour of testing! Without protection! When the smoke cleared, when the test was over (and not until the test was over), you could see that the churches remained . . . bloody, shaken, but still there!

Why had Paul not spoken out *before* this? Don't tell me he had nothing to say. Don't tell me he was surprised at what happened. Don't tell me this all came unexpectedly. There's only one reason Paul had not spoken out, corrected, warned and protected! He could not, because God *had boxed him in!* God had taken all his weapons away from him. There was nothing he could say or do—or at least nothing he could say or do *out of a pure heart.* The only pure thing he could do was remain silent, know it was going to happen, watch it happen and, in the meantime, *minister only Christ.* Hallelujah! May his tribe increase.

No, before Paul wrote the letter to the Galatian churches— that is, to Lystra, to Derbe, to Iconium and to Antioch-Pisidia— until that letter arrived and those dear saints unrolled that scroll, they were almost totally unschooled and unprepared for the coming of the circumcised or for any other ominous dangers! The content of Paul's letter to them was almost a total shock...dealing with a subject to which they had been given only the vaguest introduction.

Reread the letter. Can you reach any other conclusion?

But more!

Do you think Paul was too untalented to figure out a way to have previously warned the four churches? Why didn't he warn them? He left them open prey to the circumcision. Why?

Paul was a minister of *Jesus Christ,* not of warnings and doctrines; not of a Pauline movement. Christ was the center and the circumference of his ministry. Circumcision is not Christ. Attacking Jews is not Christ. Attacking Christians is not Christ. Preserving *his* ministry is not Christ. Building on negatives is not Christ.

Paul knew such men would probably come. But he was boxed in. Boxed in to Christ. He was not allowed to speak. Be fully warned: God makes just such demands of His workers.

Paul looked about. Tools were everywhere. Methods of all sorts lay before him. Good tools, effective tools. Pick them up and they would work: some defensive, some negative, some aggressive, some courageous. All were justifiable, but *none* were *Christ.*

Oh, the garbage we throw into a Christian's ear just to scare him off of another group. Oh, the awful things we say and do just to keep a man in our own group.

Paul lived every day in the full knowledge of what was in store for the churches. And he died daily. Loss was *his* way!

Look at his pain. You can almost feel him writhe in silent agony.

Above all . . . I carry with me – daily – the burden of all the churches.

I close by calling your attention to one last thing. Paul did not preserve his work, and for such high resolve his reward was to see men trample his work. (Further, not only did he leave his own work unguarded, he never once interfered with the territory or ministry of any other man. Not once. You could only locate Paul on the frontier.) Boxed in. Boxed in by God—left without any weapons to wage war with. Permission is granted from God to do nothing but sit, watch and wait: a silent, dumb spectator standing mute as men destroy his life's work. And in so losing, the work lived and became *indestructible.* Open your eyes; see the beauty of God in such ways.

This is how high Paul has carried the standard of the worker. Look up. There it is! At the very summit. See it? And for over a millenium, few, if any, men have reached such splendid heights. *That* is our standard. There it waves. If we are going to have a goal, let it be that one. Let us tread those heights again; this is our mission.

CHAPTER 14

Is There Scriptural Justification
for Answering Accusations?

I trust your image of Paul is crumbling. Let us look even more closely at this man. After all, he is perhaps the best known worker in church history. Men invariably quote him to justify their own conduct as workers.

I am aware that there is an almost unanimous opinion that Paul did defend himself, and therefore I am barking up the wrong fact. The best illustration is Paul's apostleship. It appears he spent a great deal of time "proving" he was an Apostle. Men will often say to you, "Defend yourself. Paul did, you know." And if you have an adversary, he will probably accost you with, "Prove you are a _____." (You may insert the word. It could be anything: "A man called of God," "A man sent by God," "A true servant of God," "A prophet," "An Apostle," etc.) He will say to you, "Prove it! Paul did!"

Paul did not!

Again, let us take a new look at the Scripture. Just when *did* Paul defend himself? Poor Paul, men are always citing him as justification of their most vicious deeds. Does Paul's life justify such justifications?

He was converted in Damascus, preached there, and was forced out of town. He moved out in the Arabian desert for several years, came back to Damascus, almost got himself killed, fled the city, tried to go to Jerusalem, fled from there, and finally went home to Tarsus for several years. Barnabus then went to Tarsus, got Paul and took him to Antioch. Paul lived in Antioch four years;

it was there he and Barnabas were sent out—made Apostles—by the Holy Spirit.

And from that moment on men raised doubts about whether or not Paul was a genuine, bona fide Apostle. And did he defend himself?

Next, Paul and Barnabas took a two year trip on which they raised up four churches. There is certainly no record of his defending himself during this time. Two years. No defense.

At home in Antioch Paul got news that the "false brethren" had invaded the four churches he and Barnabas had just raised up. He wrote a letter to the churches. The false brethren had raised grave questions among those four churches about Paul, about his gospel, who he was—*everything!* He ignored the personal attacks; he brushed aside the doubts about his apostleship with one half of a sentence, "Paul, an Apostle of Jesus Christ, not by the will of men, but the will of God." He then lunged, pen in hand, into the heart of the matter . . . the centrality of Jesus Christ. Can you say *that* was Paul defending his apostleship?

Later Paul made a second trip. This time he was better known, more controversial, and under far more attack and pressure. It was during this trip that men really began to hound his footsteps.

Well, half way through that trip he wrote a letter. (Actually two: Thessalonians.) Did he get off the subject of Christ? Did he defend himself? Read the letter. Is it a letter written on the defensive? Does it sound like a letter written by a man trying to protect his work? No, it is written in the passion of love to a church in deep trouble.

When Paul wrote that letter he had one and a half more journeys left in his life. That was all. And there is no apostolic defense in that letter. Did he start off, "Paul, an Apostle of Jesus Christ?" No. The letter began simply, beautifully, "Paul, Silas, and Timothy to the church of the Thessalonians." If he was being challenged on the issue of apostleship, it wasn't registering with him. Sorry. No defense here either.

I'm afraid you may have to go somewhere else to get your justification for defending yourself in the tight spots.

All right, let's take a new look at the one time Paul did defend his apostleship. He did, once, yes. When? At a time which he *thought* was the end of his life.

Here is the story.

Paul stood at the *close* of his *third* journey.* He was being told daily that if he went to Jerusalem he would probably be killed. As far as Paul was concerned, he was already sentenced to death.

And it was at this time, in this setting, that he wrote the incomparably beautiful letter to Corinth. In that letter, which was just about a farewell to life itself, he defended his call and his sending.

But note this: He wrote that letter to a church six years old! A church he raised up; a church where men had repeatedly challenged Paul's credentials. They had never before, in all those years, heard any of these stories . . . he had never defended himself nor his apostleship, though he was under tremendous and continued outside pressure to do so and could have eased many problems if he had. Finally, at the (supposed) end, he speaks . . . majestically! It was not so much a defense as it was ''now that it no longer matters, I will tell you things I've never told anyone.''**

And interestingly enough, he did not use that historical day in Antioch when he and Barnabas were set aside by the Holy Spirit . . . he did *not* use *that* day to prove his apostleship. He used the existence of the church in Corinth to prove his apostleship!

Take note: Paul raised up the church in Corinth, and then left it. Several years later the false brethren came to Corinth. These conniving fakers who came there for one purpose—to draw the church away from Paul—had dogged Paul's footsteps for years. He knew they would come to Corinth. He knew what they would do when they got there. But mark this: The church in Corinth didn't have the slightest idea who the men were the day they arrived in town. They had never been pre-warned by Paul. Amazing.

---

*He had been an Apostle at least *eleven years . . . and had* never *defended his apostleship during* all *this time.*

**Six years they had known him; six tumultuous years when his apostleship had been under constant attack, and in all that time the church in Corinth had never heard him defend his apostleship.*

Could you walk that way? Bear *that* cross, be *that* silent, for *that* long... with so much at stake?

Those men were Paul's greatest cross, the very heartbreak and agony of his life . . . but Corinth did not know that!!! The church in Corinth opened their arms to those men. They gave them a big money offering and believed every word the rascals said!

And that, dear reader, is one of the greatest tributes to a man in all human history. Why? Because that fact proves that Paul did not prepare his converts, did not protect his work; he did not ruin his converts with warnings. He left them to God, and gave them the privilege of *going through* a crisis — not saving them *from* a crisis. Paul knew that to do otherwise was to warp them. That is perhaps the greatest distinction between the work of Paul and the work of other men. He let crises come. And it also proves he practiced what he said he practiced ... he knew nothing among God's people except Christ. How contrary to men today who keep up a constant battle protecting the Lord's people in their own group from every shadow and hint of a crisis!

Paul, this incredible man, did not fear seeing his work tried by fire. And he kept to the subject. The *only* subject: Christ.

By the way, those men — the false brethren — said Paul had no credentials. *They* had credentials: letters from the church in Jerusalem. Paul knew the depths of his own words when he said, "Yes, I *do* have credentials! You (the church) are my credentials." Who else could produce such "letters;" churches that could stand up under, and survive, the onslaught of wolves and come out unscathed in soul, still youthful, still innocent, still believing?

The false brethren couldn't do *that!* They *couldn't* found churches ... and surely not *that* kind of a church! But Paul could! Oh, they could attack! They could fight over doctrine. They could do all the things most workers do today. Paul *couldn't do that.* He could only *minister Christ . . . and remain silent.* Yes, all Paul could do was *found churches!!! Real ones!*

Paul was saying: "I wept. I suffered. I bled. I was mistreated. But out of those losses a church was born. And soon after your birth, problems arose. Crises came roaring in like tidal waves. One, then another. And another. Wolves from without. Wolves from within. The synagogue. The Empire. Problems within. Critics, doubters, assaults, riots. And you, the church, have come through every one of them. You have survived! *You* are the proof of my apostleship.

"All of you, you who criticize her, who criticize me and damn me: Let me see *you* raise up a church—innocent, pure, loving, open, without legalism, fear or rules. Let me see you raise up a work that can stand the kind of assaults you have launched.

"Without paranoia. Fresh, alive and ready to go again. Let me see you produce such a letter. You who criticize me, damn her and seek to destroy both—where is her equal?

"Tell my critics. Tell your guests there, those who wish to see my letter, tell them I await a similar letter from them! The eight churches I have raised up have all stood. They are the proof, my only proof, of apostleship. *They* (not a prayer meeting in Antioch where the Holy Spirit spoke) are the *proof* I am sent of God."

That was Paul's defense, his only defense; and he made that defense only at what he believed to be the end of his life.

Yes, it turns out, workers *do* have scriptural right to defend themselves. Only one! Let this stand and this *alone* be your defense! Can a pure, innocent, indestructible church be *your* defense?

(Where does Paul's example leave the rest of us? Us! The workers! Sensitive, peevish, protective, defensive, bristling, ready to war at the drop of a criticism.)

Why did Paul not defend himself? For the same reason Paul did not teach the churches to look out for all the enemies, pitfalls, problems, etc., that awaited them. Why? Because such things are so much less than Christ—and a distraction from Christ.

Besides, he knew who he was! He trusted his own work! He actually believed it would stand without protection! Such a worker, greatly to be prized; who can find one?

He knew what was going to take place when he walked into a town. But in his coming, in his staying and in his departing—he said *nothing* about these things. He stood dumb. Defenseless. Nothing to throw at the problem except Christ. Only Christ.

He could have saved them so much suffering; and himself . . . pure agony. The saints could have been made aware, *and* prepared. But to bring up such a subject would have been less than Christ.

What was the result of such passive boldness . . . such willingness to suffer loss? This: On the other side of the fire emerged a woman—the church—worthy of being the very counterpart of Christ.

"I will not make you unbalanced. I will not feed you on fears, doubts and ghostly shadows. I am going to fill you with Christ. As such, you are more vulnerable. Yes, I know that one negative attack can do more than 10,000 positive words. One negation can undo a lifetime of giving men nothing but Christ. The first (Christ, only Christ) is so fragile, so destructible, so weak, so vulnerable, so easily blown away. And the other, so powerful, so overwhelming, so destructive, so irresistible, so total and all-consuming. But I will not yield. I will give you Christ. Let others give you wood, hay and stubble. And let them set a fire. And let that fire sweep the church and leave her in a rubble. EVERY MAN'S WORKS *MUST BE* TRIED. It is inescapable, inexorable. So let it come. And what is left, somewhere there in the ruins and rubble, will be a little gold, some silver and some precious stone. This is all that will be left. But *that* will be Christ."

Some of you will be workers someday. You will pass through many crises, witness much trouble. And you will learn, instinctively, a great deal; some things good, some things not good at all. You will learn how to avoid problems, how to stop crises, how to end confusions. How to con men and frighten saints. How to win. How to rule . . . how to crush threats, within and without. A thousand tools. Endless tricks. So much is at your disposal to aid you in building the house of God. Gradually those tools *will* emerge. And you *will* know how to use them.

One illustration. I observed one such tool way back as a young man in the ministry. Here! I will give you one such tool now!

Do you want to have unity? I'll tell you a way. It never fails. It works every time. Is unity threatened? You can rally the troops and bring everyone together in an instant. You can restore unity. Instantly. How?

178

Give the Lord's people a common enemy. To have unity, give a group of people a cause, and give them a common enemy. Or, in essence, teach them to hate. Give them an enemy to fear and stand against. You will have instant unity. There! A tool. It is yours. You can use it any time you need it. Just attack someone or something. A man, a doctrine, a movement—or an "instant" heresy. Create a bugaboo that is about to sweep in and swallow everyone. If you are not clear about what I mean, then read *Animal Farm*.

See how Napoleon used the name of his enemy, Snowball, to create a diversion everytime there was a crisis. Men have been doing that very thing throughout all church history. There! A much used tool! That tool is now yours, if you wish to use it.

Yes, it is less than Christ. Far, far less. And remember this: Someday your work will be tried. You can put off that day, but you can't prevent it. The day of fire *must* come.

And when the day of fire comes, what tools will you use?

May it dawn on you that all those tools at your disposal are not Christ. Each day these tools are right there in front of you. Temptations are what they really are. You will try to pick them up. (Men have used these tools for 1700 years now.) The hand of God will check you. You will be frustrated in that hour. You will cry out, "Then what shall I do?! I have nothing in my hand. Lord, You have taken *everything* away from me. I am defenseless. I am dumb. You will not even allow me to speak! Lord, not even one word? Not even a raised eyebrow?" And at that moment you will realize the Lord has *you* boxed in!

And you will realize, the church *is* going to fall. It is going to be utterly decimated. Yes, it *is* going to fall and shatter. There is no hope. This is the end. And, so many dear brothers and sisters are going to suffer irreparable damage. What will *they* do? What carnage it will be. "Yet, Lord, You will allow me to do nothing in this most dreadful of all hours! "

In that hour, that dark hour, if you are a faithful minister of Jesus Christ, you will step back and say, "All right, Lord, the church will fall. So be it. The saints will be wrecked! So be it. Lord . . . (and it is here that the center of your soul dies. It is here, at *this* point, that the hidden motives of your own black heart emerge and are dealt with) . . . my reputation and my ministry will become a laughingstock to all men. (And add this: "I'll lose my income, too!") So be it, Lord. If I cannot minister Christ—if I cannot minister Him, and that out of a pure spirit, if I must stoop to anything lower, even for an instant—I will do nothing; let it *all* fall! If I have to choose between seeing the Kingdom of God defeated or giving men less than Christ, then I will see the Kingdom defeated." Saints, seize *that* standard. What a high victory it will be when *the cross* wins!!!

CHAPTER 15

The Thorn

We are looking at the worker. We are seeking to establish a standard of conduct that will be our north star. Nowhere is the standard more clearly seen than in the story you are about to read, for it is one of the most incredible tales in all human history. It is the story of Paul and his famous thorn in the flesh. It was a great thorn, incredibly great. One day God may very well give us this exact same thorn.

Paul spoke of "dangers from false brethren." As I said much earlier, we will see what perils came from these men. We will see Paul's conduct when facing the "false brethren" type of crisis, just as we once observed his reaction to the "Jewish" crises and the "gentile" crises.

So, our story will deal with two things: Paul's *thorn* and the *"perils"* which he faced from *false brethren.* It is this story which will—more than anything else we have covered—show us what the Lord has called us to. We will see just how far, how *very* far, it is from where we are now to the top of the summit: how steep the slope, how impossible the assault. How unlikely the prospect. Yet despite the odds, we have no choice. *Here* is our call.

We will begin our story at Paul's conversion.

The Story of the Thorn

When Paul was converted, he also had a great revelation. As great, or greater, than any ever known. For one thing, at the very outset of his Christian life he knew he would be an Apostle to the gentiles. He was given a clear revelation of the Gospel. Now think about that. From God he had received such revealed knowledge. That would make any man confident. Even *over*confident. In fact, confident enough to destroy himself. That revelation, so great, contained the potential for Paul's destruction.

About ten years after his conversion, at about age forty (probably), he took up the work of apostleship. Ten years *after* the revelation. Ten years of *waiting*. Finally, he began a two-year journey with Barnabas. Four churches were raised up on that journey. Then Paul and Barnabas came home. The trip had been a blazing success. There was suffering, yes. But it was also a resounding *victory*. Just enough to make a man dangerous in the Lord's work. The specter of overconfidence and the show of pride lurked in the wings.

Would the seed of destruction, already sown in Paul, now bloom? No! For God was preparing a thorn for Paul! The full impact probably first hit Paul after he got back home to Antioch, *after* that first trip out. It was a hideous, unbearable thing which God gave him. But it accomplished its task. It made Paul weak! Broken! It cured his overconfidence . . . and it left him in knots for the rest of his life. What was that thorn? Poor eyesight? No. Something much more awesome than that.

Let's go on with the story. That first trip was over; the two men had come home to Antioch. But they were met with a problem. Someone from Jerusalem came to Antioch and created a really big crisis there. Visitors, *Christian* visitors (!) . . . from *Jerusalem* (!) were telling the Antioch Christians that they had to be circumcised to be true believers.

Now a question is in order: Who led this Jerusalem group? What was the man's name? The answer: We do not know!

The problem was serious. It was so serious that Paul and Barnabas had to make a trip to Jerusalem to get the whole thing settled. The men who came to Antioch had raised serious questions and had shaken everyone's faith. Something had to be done. These troublemakers came from the church in Jerusalem, so in that city the problem would be faced. Barnabas, Paul and a few others struck out for the Holy City!

In Jerusalem, then, men came together to solve the problem. It was the greatest assembly of spiritual giants in all history. Fourteen Apostles, the elders of the church, some Antioch Christians and "others" . . . whose names we do not know.

After a long discussion, the matter came to a head. Peter stated the solution, James confirmed it. Paul and Barnabas had been vindicated. They rejoiced: one more victory. The "gentile" gospel had taken the day. A letter would even be sent out from Jerusalem back to Antioch, and to *all* five of the gentile churches. Truly a major triumph. Those antagonistic men who had come to Antioch from Jerusalem were shown to be in error. The problem of whether or not a man had to be circumcised in order to be a believer was settled.

In actual fact, however, it had only begun.

Something else very interesting took place at that Jerusalem council. No one took any great note of it at the time, though. Some brother had come into the meeting who either didn't belong, or if he did, he did not go along with the decision. Men were present who were there "spying out" the gentile liberty (Gal. 2:4). Perhaps it was in that very meeting that this man—or group of men—resolved to dog Paul to the ends of the earth, to challenge and destroy all Paul ever said or did, wherever he went.

Enter "false brethren."

From that moment on, and for the rest of his life, though he did not then know it, there would be a devouring hound ever at his heels. So it is a mysterious, nameless man who begins to emerge in our story. But who? We don't know!

This we do know: Paul went out on yet a second journey. He revisited those four new churches. But when he got there this man had preceded him! (See the whole book of Galatians.) This man—or men—had well nigh turned all of Paul's converts into *Jewish-*Christian gatherings; he had so totally won them over to this "more enlightened" gospel of his that the people had more or less, it seems, left Paul and followed another man. Who? We don't know.

But this we do know: Paul faced a crisis. It was this: "What shall I do about this man, about the four churches; and what about all those as yet unborn churches out there in the future?''

Would he attack the man? Somewhere, sometime soon after Paul penned that Galatian letter—perhaps it was a short time later, when he went to Galatia—Paul learned firsthand what this man had said . . . saw the damage he had done . . . . It was sometime soon afterward that Paul went to the Lord and sought the Lord to take that man out of his life. After all, that man had nearly wrecked Antioch, and had come even closer to success in Galatia. Paul must have reeled in agony as God began to unfold to him what his relationship to this man must be! God was giving Paul no defendable perimeter!

(We will see later that it was also on this very same occasion that Paul received his thorn.)

And so Paul's confidence began to be shattered. The motives of his heart were being tested. His Christian graces were being tried. His "turn-the-other-cheek" gospel was being subjected to strenuous extremes. Was it real in him? Paul had been thrown in the fire. God hit him in his weak parts, his most vulnerable spot: the churches. And God began to make an unbelievable demand on Paul. The standard of the worker was being raised. And God was the one meting out the measure!

A man out there had given his whole life to seeing the gentile gospel, the gentile churches, the gentile Apostle, destroyed. The churches, those born and those as yet unborn, were facing destruction. Suddenly God boxed Paul in. Paul was made defenseless, struck dumb. All he could do was wait silently until this man struck again, and again and again. Here we begin to see a man who seeks to destroy Paul, and he is doing it with an energy that rivals Paul's own . . . yet for the opposite reason. One pours out his life to build gentile churches, the other pours out his life to destroy them.

Who was he? We do not know. But this we do know: Paul knew he would come . . . to every city . . . to every church. Every day of his life, he knew. But he did not speak! Years later—after he had tramped his way across Philippi, Thessalonica, Berea and Corinth and finally Ephesus, where he was facing certain death—

184

word reached Paul that this man had come to Corinth, just as he had come to all the other cities where Paul had raised up churches.

I have asked you, who is this man so mercilessly hounding Paul's whole life? We do not know. Paul tells us very clearly who he is, but the truth is, Paul tells us who this man is only after *years* and years of having lived with this indescribable cross.

We are discussing a nameless man. The "false brethren," no less. Now let's change the subject. Let's talk about Paul's thorn.

Paul spoke in II Corinthians of a "messenger from Satan." That is strong language from a man who gave Satan credit for little or nothing.

Let us take a closer look at this "messenger," for a surprise awaits us.

This "messenger" kept Paul humble and weak. What is this messenger which Paul calls a *thorn?* We think of Paul's thorn as an "it." But in the *very same passage* Paul speaks of a *man* who came to Corinth and "preached *another* gospel." A worker, yes, but a *deceitful* one. (See II Cor. 11:13-15) *What* is this thorn??? *Who* is this messenger??? Is Paul discussing two subjects? Or one?!

Why did God put this thorn in Paul's life? Why this cross? "Because of the sheer greatness of my revelation, a thorn was put in my flesh . . . to buffet me . . . to keep me from exalting myself."

Could the "thorn" *and* the man who "preached another gospel" be one and the same? Yes. The evidence is overwhelming. Reread II Corinthians 11:13 to 12:9. The thorn and the messenger are the *same. They* are *a man!* Here is the Wuest translation of the passage:

Concerning this [messenger] three times I begged the Lord that he might depart from me. And He has said to me, and His declaration still stands, My grace is enough for you, for power is moment by moment coming to its full energy and complete operation in the sphere of weakness.   II Corinthians 12:8-9

The most interesting thing about this particular translation is that the "thorn" is called a "he." Paul's "thorn" was a man! And three times Paul asks that God do something about this *man!* Three times God said, "It's better you be weak. Let the man do what he will. *I'll not take him away.* I'll give you grace to stand by and watch him destroy you.'' Paul, it will be your weakness which will be your strength!!!

Heads up! You who would be workers! Observe what is unfolding!

Our curiosity is now out of control. Who is this mysterious man? He has come now to Corinth and he has been so well received! We do not know who he is, but we are beginning to collect all the pieces! The answer is near. One thing is clear, *he* is Paul's thorn.

This man, whoever he was, was a worker. He was held in high esteem. He had been sent out by the Jerusalem church; consequently he had credentials from the church in Jerusalem attesting that he was a genuine, bona fide Apostle. He had now arrived in Corinth. An Apostle from Jerusalem!!! They received him, put him up, listened to him, gave him money—and believed *every* word he said.

This man, as in every previous city, managed—very subtly—to bring up grave doubts about Paul. ''All true Apostles have verifying letters. Paul doesn't, you say? . . . Paul took no love offering, you say? Hmmm, that's interesting.''

It is so obvious that the church in Corinth, though about seven years old, had *never* heard of this man and certainly had never been forewarned of him. Yet Paul lived every day of his life in dread of this man. After all, this man was clever; he wooed the church right over to himself. In fact, things were so bad Paul wasn't sure he could ever return to Corinth. Yet Paul had *never* spoken of this man's existence nor warned the church in Corinth of his dangerous and powerful gospel; nor of the destruction he had caused in Antioch, Galatia . . . and who knows where else! In seven long years of the existence of the church in Corinth they had never heard Paul refer to this man . . . this man who was the most crushing cross Paul ever knew! Mark that, dear would-be worker!

Could you walk such a straight path? Can any man?! Well, remember this: Paul did!

Who was this man? We do not know, but Paul wrote a letter to the Corinthians that finally *alluded* to his existence. The letter he wrote would probably be the last letter Paul would ever pen. He mentioned this situation—this man—at what he assumed was the very end of his ministry . . . at the end of his life.

Never forget that fact. Until this hour of almost certain death, Paul never spoke of, and Corinth never heard of, Paul's worst enemy . . . his most unbearable, unbelievable cross.

Who was this man? We do not know. But let's see if we can put the pieces together. Luke probably gives us our first hint of this man's existence when he writes about the conversion of "temple priests" in Jerusalem. (Later these priests almost gained the upper hand in the church there.) Next, we hear about a visit to Antioch by some important men from Jerusalem. Next, there are the "spies" at the Jerusalem council. After that we hear about a delegation of men who go out from Jerusalem to all four Galatian churches, and well nigh talk all the saints there into being circumcised.

These men later appear in Philippi, Thessalonica and finally Corinth.

And so the dim outline of this man emerges. Probably he is a temple priest or Pharisee; he is leading a group of men who are all converted priests or Pharisees, men who are all intent on establishing a Judaistic gospel; and later, as they observe the ascent of Paul and his gospel, they also become intent on stopping Paul, his churches and his gospel. Now, behold the thorn! And don't sell this man short. He may very well have been a highly respected, very gifted and, perhaps, well known man. That he had charisma is beyond debate.

Who is this man? We do not know. Mark this: One of the greatest tributes ever paid a Christian must be paid to Paul . . . . What tribute? That we do not know this man, his name or anything else. It is all lost. Forever. But the fact is, the man was Paul's arch-enemy. Paul never mentioned him. Paul lived *above*. He lived *above* the grizzliest cross ever placed on him.

Is it possible, even conceivable, that this man had been following Paul so long, and that Corinth was totally unprepared for his arrival? Unprepared. Unwarned about this man; so much so that Corinth put him up, heard him, paid him, believed him and followed him?!! Is that possible? At the end of a decade of this man's marauding brother Paul, Corinth didn't even know this man existed? Yet he was intent on destroying all of Paul's ministry!

If that be true, then why did Paul leave the church so vulnerable? Just why had Paul never spoken of this man?

Well, was Paul so unskilled that he couldn't figure out how to stop this man, or so unwise that he didn't think to forewarn the church? Impossible!!!

Or, are we wrong? Perhaps Paul *did* warn the churches beforehand that a subtle Judaizer would probably arrive soon after he departed.

"Surely he did!" To do otherwise would border on *madness.*

But don't forget, we are dealing with *divine* life! And Paul was a boxed in man. God had Paul shut up, unarmed, defenseless. Day after day, year after year, Paul stood there facing his arch-enemy. Far worse than the synagogue Jews and the Roman Empire—here is a *brother,* but a *brother* who is set on the destruction of Paul, the gentile churches and the gospel. "Perils from false brethren!" Yes, *here* was Paul's peril.

What must it have been like to Paul that day when he saw what God had put in his life? Did he determine to fight this man, or warn the churches of this danger? Perhaps he would have in the earlier stages of his apostleship, back during the time of his first journey. At that time his success, his pride and his high revelation just might have caused him to be that "strong." But not anymore.

No, *God* would not allow Paul the luxury of being sidetracked; sidetracked into lower things: defenses, accusations, innuendos, writing pamphlets against enemies, etc. God checkmated Paul; he could not raise up a people nurtured on negatives, nor dispense a diet less than Christ. All Paul could do was stand there, time and time again, and watch everything he ever did be devoured.

This is the reason you find only *one* Galatian letter by Paul. It was right after he wrote that white-hot letter that God gave Paul his thorn, and therein He forever broke the "fight" in Paul.

Paul was so shut up. All he could do was go into a city, raise up a church, leave (without warning of this man) . . . and wait. Waves of opposition rolled in on him, and on an innocent, child-like, unsuspecting, unprepared people. Paul had but one thing he could do: He could weep. Day after day. Tears. That was his only defense, his only weapon.

Outwardly, he looked like a fool. But on the inside, what Paul could see, and what men who lived then and what men who live now cannot see . . . were ways that are beyond the ways of men!

"Let no man think me a fool, yet [if you must] then as a fool receive me."

What a man! Just look. See how little room God gave Paul. In the raising up of the church and in preserving it, he was allowed only the absolute minimums: As to *time, six months* in each city, usually no more. Often less. As to *preparing* them for coming *dangers*, few, if any, warnings. As to his *message*, only a positive one: Christ . . . and the cross. Powerful, yet so fragile, when later confronted with the far greater magnetism and drawing power of *negatives*. No built-in safety measures. No margin for errors. A frail work at best. One puff, and gone!!! Wow, *these* were God's limits placed on Paul.

Please remember these things.

The Results of the Thorn

But, oh, just read what Paul could say as a result. (The following Scripture *is* the same passage as the one on the thorn.) *Here* is what God was after. Oh, so unlike the thinking of workers today. Here is the *real* strong man of God!!!

"Most gladly, therefore, will I glory in my weakness . . .for when I am weak, then I am strong."

"Dear brother Paul, turn around. Look back down that road you just traveled over to arrive at this new city. A man will one day come down that same road. A powerful man. Gifted. With papers. A former temple priest, he. A powerful testimony: 'Converted from the priesthood to Christ.' In Jerusalem! Paul, that man once followed you to Antioch. Was he there in the room at the Jerusalem council? Or was he the one who went to the four churches in Galatia while others of his cohorts went to Jerusalem? 'Perils from false brothers.' A messenger from Satan, a false Apostle. He is in your life Paul; an instrument of Satan, to get you off course; to hurt you, embitter you, to make you old, to make you negative, defensive; to force you to spend time in the churches dwelling on fears, dangers and shadows, to make the church introverted, paranoid.

"He has been sent into your life to tempt you to attack another man!"

"But I will not yield. I *will* preach Christ, minister Christ, serve Christ to all men. I will be an *able* minister of Christ; nothing but Christ. God has stripped away—or taken away—all else. Take Christ out of my message, my daily conversations, and I have nothing to say.

"I will not speak against that man. You may learn less than Christ from someone, but not from me."

How would you liked to have had Paul's thorn? See him: called to raise up gentile churches; revelation beyond revelation; going out and getting himself beaten with rods; whipped, stoned, clubbed; lied about; cheated; working every day in the heat with his hands, not taking a cent; seeing the truth of his life and message distorted; hated by unbelievers and believers; and because of the atmosphere this created, doubted by the very saints on whom he poured out his soul, and for whom he suffered so. How would you like to be Paul? How would you like to stand on that road, knowing (in the face of the totality of your sacrifice) that a man will come down that same road one day and wreck everything you have ever done? And furthermore, you must go on to the next town and suffer as you did here, and with the knowledge that this work, too, will be ripped to pieces by that man. And *you* can say nothing and do nothing. Your only weapon is Christ; you are dumb to all else.

What a thorn! What a weakness! What a God! It is He who placed the thorn there! What a demand! What a standard!

"I will not criticize that man, nor even mention him. Nor will I correct, nor warn. *And in THIS, my overwhelming weakness, my*

190

Lord, You who put this limit on my life, You will have to do all else!"

When Paul said to the believers, "Imitate me," they knew he practiced his own words to the outer edges of rationality. And they were hard pressed to find justification or example to do anything else. Paul was an example. The price he paid to be that example was paid in blood. If you wait to attack someone, based on Paul's example, you'll wait a long time. As I said, one of the greatest tributes ever paid a man is paid to Paul when we see that the name of the man who went about to destroy Paul's ministry—Paul's living, breathing thorn—the greatest cross Paul ever bore—that man's name is lost to us forever. So are the names of all his cohorts. *Now* listen to Paul's words:

"Imitate *me.*"

I believe Paul was tempted to rip into that man. So, too, will you be . . . someday . . . somewhere! But Paul inventoried his heart. He dealt honestly with his hidden motives. Further, he stopped to listen for instruction from his spirit. The Spirit gave him permission to do what? Nothing! Except be destroyed. "Imitate me." *Some* cross! Some destiny!

Paul did not give in to the worker's cardinal sin: rationalizing vicious attacks on others! He did *not* give in to the rationalizing that pours in on a man—any man—in a crisis. He admitted the hidden motives of the heart, and then went in the opposite direction of them!

Just where was Paul's wellspring, anyway?

Paul worked for a living; he took no money for ministry. He ministered, suffered, sacrificed. He built, but with the knowledge that what he built would be ripped down. What was the driving motive behind all this? Nothing! That's what he got out of it all. Paul's motive, his wellspring, was his motiveless passion for Christ.

He said, "I will know YOU, and I will know You crucified." And Paul? He got nothing but the cross. Hallelujah.

Well, it took a long time, and a lot of testing, trials, suffering, plus time and then even *more* time, to produce a *worker* like that. It will take a lot more of the same, in our age, to have such men on earth . . . in your lifetime, I trust. Where is the standard of the worker? There it is, on the summit!!! Paul put it there! In agony. In blood. In suffering. With glory, he put it there! And that feat has not, perhaps, been matched since his day.

Your Mission?

Can you walk as he did? Well, be sure of this: *You will have your chance!* In that hour, may neither reason, nor logic, nor rationalization, nor common sense prevail, but the cross. May loss, not gain, succeed.

Should *this* be your lot: hungry, thirsty, beaten, imprisoned, penniless, hated and misunderstood by virtually everyone, having poured out the last measure of devotion on the church, may you consent, before the altar of God, to see all you've done crushed . . . destroyed . . . just so that you might speak negatively of no one. What a bloody price to pay; and for what? For such a small principle of conduct? Yet to so order your life as to live by this standard: "Is this Christ that I am about to minister? If not, then I shall not minister!"

Now stop a minute. You are not workers. Not now! Most of you never will be. But you are *brothers and sisters.* And this should be your conduct with one another, here in the church, and always, at all cost to you! For all your life. Be you worker or not! Why? Because one day you gave your heart to learn from the hand of God—to take not one step that is other than Christ.

It will be a long, agonizing learning. He alone can do it. But this *you* can do: You can give your *heart's motive* to such a high walk with God.

Those early believers, worker and simple saint alike, found no example in Paul that allowed them to *criticize.* And precious little example to *defend.* Today there are no workers among us—not one. There are only young men. Where do you begin? You begin in your daily life. You don't start later, out there when you get to be a worker. You start *now* with your *roommate,* with all the saints in the Lord's house! You begin here, no matter what they say or do.

192

No matter how harsh or cutting. You die (quickly) in the face of any assault. Learn that lesson *now*.

You are only a Christian experiencing the church. But someday, somewhere, the Lord will make *some* of you workers. *Woe be that day.* And someday, somewhere, the Pauline crisis will come. To you! You had better be well practiced at *losing* on that day. If not, on that day you will keep, and having kept, you will destroy.

Perhaps, by grace given to you, you will lose . . . and *be* destroyed. And from that awful, horrid, catastrophic loss, *God* will gain.

God must work, beginning now, to get some men who have nothing to present except Christ and nothing to gain except loss . . . loss of *all* things . . . including their entire life's work.

Some of you in this room will be workers. And you will face that time when you are number one in a work. And there *will* come a time when others will be out to destroy you. If not that, it may be that one day you will find yourself *under* the number one man; and one day you may wake up to find he has decided to destroy *you!* (Or you may be under the number one man who *thinks* you are out to destroy him.) Or some bizarre situation none of us can conceive of right now. Workers do clash: across tables, or across nations or sometimes even when separated by oceans. Workers come to perilous hours.

What will you be in that hour? A Luther? A Darby? Or any of the others I can call to mind—a Zwingli? Or will you be that rare exception? Will you pay the price to be a *Paul?*

If you dare walk that upward path, then ultimately you will be brought to the point that your conduct, your speech and your heart are nothing but Jesus Christ in *all* situations . . . regardless of what is taking place around you.

Look up that mountain one more time! Could you have ever dreamed a banner could have been staked so high? To reach *that* summit, *again,* to live at *that* altitude, by *that* standard, at *all* costs and *all* loss—to have such a breed of men again, *that* is our mission.

CHAPTER 16

What Happens to Men
Who Live by Divine Life?

I would like to change the subject now. I have talked about what kind of workers men must become . . . among us. But that subject is not my burden. It is not only workers who must walk this way, but it is all of us! Then why did I speak of workers? Because if they do not walk in this high way, no one else will. If they do, others will also.

So you see, all of us—workers or not—must walk a hard and difficult way. In fact, we must walk the *divine* way. The divine way is what is needed; it is the missing way. But don't think it is the exciting way or the joyous way. What is this *divine way* which we must walk? What is walking divinely? Where does it lead?

I have said to you often that we have two lives in us: human life and divine life. Before we were saved we always lived by the life form of the human. After we are saved we have another form of life in us. But more. God has made it possible for us to live by this divine life—just as we once lived by human life. We can live by divine life just as God lives by divine life.

A brother once said something rather incredible to me. It went like this: "You are really helping the saints here to learn to live by divine life. One day they will really know how to live by God's life. They will live by divine life and not by human life. But be prepared: When they do, they will begin to challenge you."

Is this true? Is that the ultimate end of living by the life of God? That's a good question. What is the ultimate end of living by divine life? Let us see. What really does await you out there if you truly live by the life of God? What can you anticipate to be your ultimate destiny if you live by the same life *God* lives by? THIS:

The ultimate result of a man living by divine life is *crucifixion!* Live by the highest life long enough and it will get you the cross. You will find out what it means, really means, to be crucified. No, you will not, as has been said, go out and overthrow somebody. That just isn't divine life conduct! The ultimate expression of divine life in you is crucifixion. *Your* crucifixion!

The first time I ever spoke in Isla Vista, I spoke on living by divine life. It was a new idea to everyone (despite the fact that it is one of the central themes of Scripture). It sounded like great fun. It sounded like a much better idea than living by human life. Well, it isn't. Remember, to live by divine life is to move toward crucifixion.

I recall my days in evangelistic work. Tinsel. Crowds. The V.I.P. treatment. Well, it's better that you stick with *that* life. I recall vividly that since I left *that* life, absolutely *nothing* has worked right. The fun ended.

Let's say you make a clear break with the world and its *ways.* Let's say you have a real heart for the Lord. Wonderful. We are a scrubby bunch. Gentiles all. Highly qualified to be gentiles. But if you fall under *the Lord's* discipline you will become gentiles who are *transformed.* The world is waiting for such an event.

Well, let's just imagine your progress.

You first enter into the practical expression of the body of Christ. Gradually, daily, you experience the Lord. Daily you behold Him. Little by little He works Himself into you. You learn to deny the very essence of your self. You learn something of the working of the Lord's Spirit in your spirit. You begin to learn to live by a life not your own.

One day you come to a hard place in the road. You look up. There is the cross. By His grace you pass through it. Then the Lord takes you farther on, from one plane to another. (Sometimes He also goes *back,* to replay lessons you may have just barely learned, or *almost* learned. They're called "review lessons.") Each rung gets harder; the dealings of God are deeper with each passing year. Let me illustrate.

I wish all of you to know that the dealings you are going through are all rather shallow dealings. The Lord is dealing with you about . . . oh, let's say about transportation. There you are. You want a car. A very particular car. My, do you ever want that car. You are driven, obsessed. Every turn of your intestines screams, "I've got to have *that* car!" You can't live without it. But God can. The two lives battle. Finally you come to the Lord, and with every cell in your body screaming in protest, the car is surrendered to your Lord.

What next? Well, sometimes I've fancied a heavenly IBM computer. The record of the above event is fed into it, there is a moment's pause, then comes a new read-out: "This one is now ready for a bigger encounter with the cross." And so God takes you on higher . . . and the cutting of the cross goes deeper and deeper. This is the upward experience of learning to live by divine life.

Get prepared. Somewhere out there in the not-too-distant future awaits another, greater experience of the cross. Actually, what it really is is a greater opportunity for you to turn to Christ, rather than turning to your own ways.

If enough years pass (and you had better believe it will take *many* years), the things going on between you and the Lord can get mighty weighty—you may sense only the slightest moving of God in you, but it will be over the most cataclysmic, important and highly refined issues. The enounter with the cross ever enlarges . . . the *way* to walk becomes *less* clear.

Folks drop in on us so often from all over the country, look around, and say something to the effect of, "Gee, what a beautiful accident." They do not know what we have been through. And *we* don't know what we will *yet* go through!!! This we know: The Lord must take us beyond where we are. That, of necessity, demands greater suffering. The body of Christ must be constantly filling up the sufferings of Christ.

Follow the Lord long enough and that IBM print-out will one day not only say, "He is ready for a bigger cross," it will also say, "It is time he be crucified." *That* is where someone who lives by divine life ends up!

The cross is laid there in front of you; at your very feet. Men are waiting. Waiting to drive in the nails. But you must render up the work . . . you must render up your will. You stare at the cross for a moment. You lean forward. You grasp it. You turn. You lie down; you stretch out your arms. You open your hands. And you await the nails.

Thank God. Do it. But be warned. You will be called on to do this more than once. Once. Then again. And again. Then one day you make a startling discovery. You look back on a life of loss. Then you see! The Lord takes care of everything. It finally dawns on you Whom it is you serve. Finally, the realization breaks in on you with brilliance: "Unless the Lord builds the house, they labor in vain who build it."

Paul said, "Imitate me." The worker is going to be imitated. Look at Paul. See his standard. Imitate that standard! Imitate this high, exotic standard. Here is *your* mission.

Two Men Who Lived by Divine Life

I have said that if you live by divine life long enough, the end result will be crucifixion.

Let me illustrate that fact through the lives of two people who lived in the first century. The first is Paul. He grew and grew in divine life. It brought him a crucifixion. (Yes, strong tradition says he was beheaded. Nonetheless, he was *crucified.*)

Observe the life of Paul as it evolved from one depth to another. See him at *first:* the new convert; you can sense the zeal, the boldness. These are the greatest characteristics of the man. *Later,* see him as the man "sent" by the Holy Spirit. Next there come the physical hardships: suffering, tears, hunger, cold. As the divine life increases, the road gets steeper; physical hardships turn into beatings, whippings, stones, rods, jails, dungeons, shipwrecks. To these beatings is added the agony of the burden for the churches: distraught, fearful for their sakes; sheer, endless, doubled-up agony.

The divine life increases with every rung ascended and with

every suffering embraced. Now, toward the end, the agonies multiply. There is a delegation of men traveling behind him, wherever he goes. International travelers, spreading destruction . . . and they have a full-time commitment to their task: destroy Paul's work!

And Paul? It was hard adjusting to his new, harder role. He almost didn't make it several times. But see him. He bears it all, all of it, daily—not one thundering storm assailing him, but a deluge of storms. *This* is where living by divine life has gotten Paul! He bears the cross daily. Will it finally end? Rest, at last? No! What happens is the very opposite. Always! God raises the stakes even higher.

One day comes the print-out: "Paul is ready to be crucified." Divine life is seasoned, aged and embedded. The final test is made ready. Divine life always ends up being challenged to express itself *here*. And it is also the *nature* of divine life to be brought to this test. The test? Can the divine life *embedded* in you, *born* in you, *one* with you, be the life that is in control during a public crucifixion?

And so Paul's day arrived. His faithfulness, his ever growing deeper spiritual life—where did it bring him? To an ugly, horrendous, vicious crucifixion.

Yet, oh, oh, oh, what a testimony is left to us as a result. What a demonstration of what divine life is like when it is being lived out in a man. What an awesome glimpse of how divine life conducts itself! It is so utterly unlike the way human life conducts itself. How utterly opposite to all we understand. How totally at variance with the whole record of church history.

Here is the story.

You recall from earlier illustrations that on his third trip Paul went to Ephesus. He was in that area about four years. Then he left. His destination? Jerusalem! And certain death. He went by way of several side trips (one to Corinth), some planned, some not planned. Finally, he got to Palestine. He stopped in cities along the way. Everyone begged him not to enter Jerusalem. Agabus as good as predicted his death. But Paul was determined.

Look around. The future couldn't be darker. Paul has won a reputation with the Roman Empire that now reaches from Jerusalem to Corinth. He is in trouble with the Romans. Secondly, the unbelieving Jews are after him everywhere. A sect called "daggermen" sprinkled throughout the whole Empire have put into motion a plan to locate him, ambush him and kill him. Thirdly, there are the "false brethren," of whom we spoke before, who have now entered every church Paul has raised up. Their campaign to discredit him in the gentile churches is in full swing. These churches totter on the balance: They could go either way.

The thing that is really destroying Paul (i.e., destroying his effectiveness, his reputation, making him suspect to absolutely everyone, closing all doors to him, about to make him a social outcast) is the whole, huge mess in concert. He is feared by Romans, hated by Jews, dogged, lied about and defamed by false brethren. Lastly, it is being flung in his face—and proclaimed to all the gentile churches—that he is out of favor in the church in Jerusalem. If that be true, then he is "outside the faith." Who would want to get near Paul at a time like this? This is obvious: Most of the believers are simple-hearted people; people who will walk a mile out of the way to avoid *any* pressure situation. They are people who don't want to live out their lives in turmoil just for the sake of following a fellow that nearly everyone considers wrong! Could it be that Paul is the only one who is right? Unlikely. And the rumors! There are so many, and they are so titanic. What if even a few are right??! And some must surely be true.

Paul was fast losing his footing everywhere on earth. He was on the verge of being destroyed. By his own testimony (II Corinthians), this was the blackest hour of his life.

Paul knows (taking a quick look into the not-so-distant future —although at the moment this has definitely *not* yet happened) that, given a little more time, his converts will not even be regarded as true followers of Christ; the gentile churches will not be considered churches at all!

One last thing to add insult to injury. And I believe this one galled Paul more than all the other hardships combined during his whole ministry. Paul was picking up a brand new rumor everywhere: "Paul doesn't know the Scripture." *This* story was being passed on to *his* converts. And some were believing it. It was being parrotted by everyone. The part that stung the most was to be hearing it coming from the lips of men who did not know the Scripture one-tenth as well as he, men who only thought they knew it; they even thought *he* should be taught by them because he was so ignorant. After all, if what he said was new to them, it must be false. It never occurred to them that his ministry was only revealing *their* ignorance. Truly, ignorance had reached new depths. Nevertheless, Paul was hurt deeply. Inside he was angry and dumbfounded. This was the ultimate shame.

It was with this backdrop that Paul reached Jerusalem. He had felt he had to go. These tensions had been fermenting and brewing for years. The cork was about to pop. Paul was determined to go to the church in Jerusalem, armed with a huge gift of money for the needs of the local saints, thereby proving to them once and for all that he and the gentile churches were one with Jerusalem . . . even if it cost him his life. He knew that the solving of this problem was of paramount importance to the survival of the faith.

Paul had brought along with him some very dear young men. All were from gentile churches. One of these young men was named Tychicus.

Paul met with the church leaders. They accepted the gift. But the situation was too grave for a gift to solve. They gave him an overview. "The whole city knows you are here. The atmosphere is charged. The orthodox Jews hate you. The 'more-Hebrew-than-Christian' believers despise you. The faithful are either wary or confused. Many feel you are here to destroy the traditions of the past and to tear down the teachings of Moses."

They offered a solution. "Take a Mosaic vow. Some of the other saints here in the church are just about to start one. Join them. This will prove to everyone you are an orthodox follower of Moses."

Paul agreed. (Fantastic!) He forthwith had his entire head shaved. (And I have a notion that half a dozen young gentile prophets stood there in speechless awe.) *"This* is the man who wrote that scorching letter to Galatia???'' Paul can surprise you. His liberty went in *both* directions. (The liberty to be legalistic! Or was it something else? Perhaps it was Paul's respect for local authority. He had been asked by the local elders to do this, and he had submitted to them!)

Paul went to the temple. He began the rites. There he was in the company of some Jewish young men, all with shaved heads. One of those men, at least when hairless, must have looked like Tychicus. Some Jews had spotted Paul giving his young gentile companions a guided tour of Jerusalem a few days before. (It must have been some tour: Paul guiding gentiles through Jerusalem, pointing out the Old Testament types, symbols and pictures of Christ and the church!)

The Jews thought Paul, now making sacrifices within the temple, had brought gentiles into that sacred place and desecrated the holy things of God. They had believed their own rumors.

A riot broke out. Its intent? To rip Paul to pieces. And it was about halfway there when a Roman garrison succeeded in penetrating the mob and seizing Paul. But he wasn't a whole lot better off. The captain of the guard thought he had just captured a famous anti-Rome revolutionary. Two groups had hold of one man, and both thought him unworthy of life.

This scene was to become one of the great tragicomic scenes of all history. Paul, bloody, beaten, dragged, pulled, pushed, clothes ripped, dirty, half-dead . . . . The Romans seized him and began trying to figure a way to get him out of there. The mob was in a rage, the Romans little better. Now, in all this, what is going through Paul's head? Look at him. His lips are swollen, his bald head is covered with blood and glistening in the sun . . . . Probably it is with the one eye he can see out of that he gets a glimpse of the gigantic crowd at the foot of the stairs, and he says to himself, "My, what a huge crowd to preach the gospel to." Somehow he beguiles the soldiers into putting him down and letting him speak to that crowd! (Maybe Paul was trying to pull off another Pentecost.) And sure enough, Paul, standing there more dead than alive, lets fly with an evangelistic invitation!

Eventually the crowd went mad at one of his typical (teensie-weensie), off-the-cuff evangelistic lampoons! Somehow the soldiers got him out of there alive. That night a group of Jews met and in solemn ceremony vowed never to eat another bite of food until Paul was dead. "Either he dies or we die!" All of my Christian life I have wondered what happened to those men. Every one of them was more than ready to see Paul die. But I venture that not one of those men was willing to see himself die.

(By the way, this is a good picture of what people who hold onto their pet doctrine are capable of doing—they commit murder! Do not say religious men will not. Every page of church history for the last seventeen hundred years says it is a fact. Church history! The record of Christians murdering Christians over doctrine!)

Paul was smuggled out of the city by the Romans to prevent his assassination.

Paul was incarcerated in the city of Caesarea. A trial was called. Down from Jerusalem paraded the temple priests, led by the high priest, arriving in their pompous robes—the fathers of all the costumed clergy that have followed them down through the ages.

The hearing begins. Here are the same men who crucified Christ, and who stoned Stephen. And here is that same scene. Religion, knowledge, legalism, decked out in pomp, threatened by one lone figure dressed in peasant's clothes. *MAY IT FOREVER BE!* Just as when they faced Jesus and Stephen, their intent is the same. The religious sages of the century are there with one thing in their hearts: *murder!* Their words are pious, their tone holy, their stated intention high sounding. "We ask that you send Paul to Jerusalem to be fairly tried by us over a religious issue." The truth is, though, they never expect the trial to come off. Their intent is that Paul never reach Jerusalem alive.

"Sound doctrine." "Defenders of the faith." And Paul, pulverized, swollen, bruised, sick and with nearly two decades of abuse from these men under his tunic, had to stand there and watch the whole hypocritical scene, with *his* life at stake!

And this, dear brother, is where divine life leads you: to a crucifixion!

One after another, they speak. False witness after false

witness; they break *their own laws* to destroy one who they believe does not accept those laws! Like Christians being unchristian to stop other Christians who don't believe as they believe.

Paul is allowed to speak. The time has come. This is the fourth man this very group would crucifiy. Jesus stood silent. Stephen preached Christ. Peter (the one who got away) slept! But this man is Paul, the tough guy. What will he do at *his* crucifixion? Enough is enough. Their lies should be exposed. Their hypocrisy should be revealed. A decade or two of this is enough. Now Paul will vent all the pent-up feelings, all the hurts and lies and suffering in one vast blast of revenge. The time has finally come. Is not this the hour to respond? (And please remember, you pious ones out there who talk about "so much is at stake and right principles must be stood for"—this man Paul has nothing less at stake than his neck.) Paul opens his mouth. And like an angel who drops out of heaven on his first visit to earth, Paul stands up there, *without a past,* and preaches the gospel of salvation . . . like a brand-new convert giving his testimony for the first time. *Not one word* of accusation about anybody or anything. What a standard. Before you take action in a time of crisis, place *your* standard beside this measuring rod.

In the midst of a crucifixion, he never bobbled. And in that titanic reach, he claimed new heights; he put to shame every man in church history who has ever attacked another person. If any man, ever, anywhere, at any time, ever had a right to attack, it was Paul, and it was *now.* None of us . . . I repeat, none of us has ever been abused like that man. We never have. I can't conceive that we ever will. Paul found no excuse to speak a word of criticism. It was as though he had just been born. Fresh, new, with no memory of past things, he waded into an evangelistic appeal to believe in Jesus Christ. What a man! What an incredible man!

Two or three times Paul went through just such disgraceful public hearings. His entire ministry was spent living in the presence of one ever-present, all-consuming lie—in cities, in homes, in the gatherings of the church. Even the reason for his being in jail was a travesty of justice. He was there only because his incarcerators hoped he would bribe his way out, so they could make money off of a man they knew to be falsely accused and unjustly imprisoned.

Go back and check the record. Read all of his words. Read Luke's biography of his life. Can you find bitterness? Any evidence of *scars?* Even in the midst of the worst personal insults, this man, this worker, walked and talked as though such bloody things had never happened. Paul had no past. He had no present. He lived outside of time. He lived above the clouds. Until *this very hour* we are not even sure exactly what it was that men accused him of in the gentile churches. His past and present were the Lord.

This is not the way human life conducts itself. You are looking straight into the face of the *one,* the *only* form of life that acts this way, under these circumstances. You are looking straight into the face of divine conduct. Get clear! Paul did not start off his Christian life with these attributes. It took years. They were woven into his experience. It took a lot of different events, a multitude of varied experiences: pain, suffering, loss . . . incalculable loss. It took embracing that cross, experiencing the Lord, living by the Lord's life. He grew up to *this point* by bearing the cross in many places, in many ways, until finally he won the right to be crucified!

What have we learned here? We have learned that God needs a new breed of servants, a new breed of Christians; men who are sufferers. But it will take a lifetime of bearing the cross, of *muted* suffering, of unjust treatment . . . without retaliation, without defending or being defensive. A lamb led to the slaughter. To work, to serve, without pay. Experiencing the extremities of human expenditure. Cold, nakedness, hunger, sleepless nights, beatings, lies at the hands of believers and unbelievers. *All* so that the church may be raised up. Beautiful, young, innocent. Yet the man *never* building into the church any mechanism for survival. Never teaching them such things. Never preserving the work of his hand. To do it all, yet doing it with the knowledge that he will certainly lose it all through the deeds of unfair, unscrupulous men!

A Review

We have learned here that men ought never to place doctrine

above fellowship. To protect a work is proof that there is no apostleship. To fight an enemy is proof that men build in fear. To preserve a work is to admit you built with nothing but wood, hay and stubble. To fight your destroyers is to prove you have no confidence in what you yourself built. To work, to build, to leave without fortifications, to raise not one finger, is to testify to the world that you believe you were engaged, not in your own work, nor in the work of men, but that you were engaged in God's present work upon the earth. For His alone is the indestructible work of the ages. For if your Lord builds not the House, those who build it labor in vain.

Now let us move on.

Another Man Who Lived by Divine Life

I want us to look at a second example.

There is another man in the New Testament age who lived by divine life. He lived *only* by divine life!!! He lived by it so completely that it got Him crucified. His name? Jesus Christ, the Son of God. *He* lived by the life of God. He kept the soul in subjection to the Spirit. He lost. "He who loses his soul shall gain it." Live by God's life long enough, and God will bring you to a point where you get a chance to choose to be crucified, or to escape crucifixion.

Now hear this: We all have human life. Right? But if we are saved we also have divine life in us. One of those lives, human life, will never agree to willingly go to the cross. Human life will try to find a way out. In fact, there is only one life form in the universe that willingly goes to the cross. Only one that acquiesces to public crucifixion. There is only one life that says, "Yes." Divine life!

Yes, it is true. Thousands of people have been crucified. But they were dragged there. Only one life form goes there without coercion.

But, did He? Didn't Jesus get in a situation where He was forcibly executed? Absolutely *not*. Just consider all the possibilites He had of escaping that crucifixion.

206

First, He had the angels He could call on. But He had less dramatic, very down-to-earth ways, too. *He could have opened His mouth.* Here is a principle: Open your mouth, and you will escape crucifixion. Just by opening your mouth, you can escape almost *any* crucifixion.

This was one of the keenest disappointments of all to the disciples. Their Lord didn't defend Himself at the trial. They found out they had a leader . . . a king . . . who wouldn't fight.

I have been in the ministry since I was eighteen years old. That's been a long time. I have observed something: a gleam in men's eyes. They love to follow a brave man, even a *tough guy.* Christians love to hear a man stand up behind a pulpit and tell stories of how he got caught in this awful situation and how he fought his way out. He had all these opponents and he fought—by George—and they all turned and ran—by George—and "I'm tough, see—by George." Men boast in their bravery.

And Christians love it. They eat it up, especially young people. "The man I follow is tough. He stands for principles. No coward is he. He defends the right, and fights the wrong and attacks those good-for-nothing buzzards."

In my whole life I can hardly recall an exception to this. Tough, fearless men. (Oh, I know there are cowards among the Lord's servants. More of them than the "brave" ones. But people only follow brave men.) My question is: Where are the *meek?!* "Meek," I say; not "cowards." Where is the man who is fearless, who is "tough," who *can* fight back and who *can* win the battle, but *who does not;* instead, he allows the cross. *That* is meekness. Where is *this* man?

Jesus severely disappointed his disciples because of His meekness at a moment they expected Him to show those lousy hypocrites a thing or two. Thank God, He didn't. Christianity, in the last 1700 years, has slaughtered enough fellow believers *without* the Lord's example to cite. I shudder to think what they might have done—by sword and fire—if they had had an example, even a *small* one!

You see, until that hour men had never watched *divine life* face the cross. They had only seen human life go to the cross. They only had human life as a rule of thumb to go by. Here was brand new conduct by a totally different form of life. A new dimension was being added to human experience. They *naturally* expected divine life (after all it was *divine life)* to fight. It was a very *logical* supposition. But it was wrong.

Yes, the Lord Jesus Christ could have stopped the proceedings! Do you doubt He could have thrown that whole Jewish trial (the *religious* trial) into an uproar? Don't underestimate Him. And the civil trial? See Jesus before Pilate. Pilate almost begged Jesus to give him a reason, any reason, for stopping the crucifixion. Jesus needed *only* open his mouth.

If you want to know what a man is really like inside, watch him as he is being attacked and slandered by others. Watch him when his job, his reputation, his life's work is being ripped down. Watch how he takes to a crucifixion!

Only divine life can bear it with nobility . . . and with silence!

There is one more thing. Look who sent the Lord Jesus to the cross. *Divine life* sent Christ to the cross. Divine life seems to be inexorably drawn to the cross. It is an innate thing. The author of divine life sent His Son to the cross, and *counted it good!*

Now watch *divine* conduct. It doesn't look very human, does it? Through the whole proceeding the Lord Jesus never defended Himself. In fact, He hardly opened His mouth. About the only time He did was when the high priest "adjured" Him by the living God. Then the Lord had to answer. He had so little to say in the face of His crucifixion.

Learn to live by the Lord's life. It's your God-given life. But please keep in mind: You are almost certainly headed for a crucifixion. Yours! A hard spot in the road is out there. A thing totally unfair awaits you. And know this: There *is* a way out. You can get out. Talk your way out. When attacked, respond, defend, thrust, talk, fight, rip. But know this: Something deep inside you is trying to get your attention. *"I* would have you be silent. I would have you go right through it."

All the way to Calvary
With my Savior I would go.
Help me, Lord, to go with Thee
All the way to Calvary.

A deep sense says, "Yes, it will hurt. But go. And as you do, go as a lamb to the slaughter." You go. And when you get there, you play no games. You use *none* of the tools available to you. No grandstanding. No short cuts. No compromises. Asking no sympathy, taking none of the easy ways. You just go.

I believe it was on my second trip to California that someone took Helen and me to Forest Lawn. There is a painting there. I believe they claim it to be the world's largest. The painting is a vast portrait of the crucifixion. The artist shows Christ looking up at the cross. It depicts, I believe, His willingness to be crucified. The probable truth is, though, that the cross was laid on the ground. A man had to be forced down onto it, then nailed to it, then lifted up into the sky.

The Lord was not forced. He stood there a moment and looked at that hideous thing lying there on the ground. Slowly, He bent down, stretched out His hands and laid Himself down, then opened the palms of His hands . . . and waited! At long last, the consummation of crucifixion. And now more than ever before, He utters not one word, neither offers any resistance. The nails are placed on *open* palms. He is willingly crucified.

This is *your* example. *Here* is how to go to the cross. Never forget it. This is divine conduct. And a call to walk *this* way: *That* is our mission.

It is an interesting thing. Live by the Lord's life and eventually you will end up being crucified. But just as interesting is this fact: Those who get crucified have a tendency to rise from the dead.

Paul and Stephen, like their Lord, went through the public ordeal of being villified, and they went through it like they weren't even there. Like they were somewhere else. Then came a resurrection. *But* resurrection is reserved exclusively for those who have taken the cross.

In order to rise from the grave you first must go to the cross. Stay alive if you wish, but for you there is no resurrection. Frankly, I have a notion the Lord would like to get most of us—maybe all of us—put through a public, ignominious, unfair crucifixion. And then He wants to raise us from the dead. The whole purpose of crucifixion: resurrection!

209

Please notice the Lord's conduct *after* resurrection. Did you notice that He finally spoke out? Did you read His scathing denunciations of all those dirty, lying, hypocrites? Did you see His bitter, boiling, venom finally unleashed on those who crucified Him? Have you read His words as He vividly outlined the trial, quoted every lie told about Him, making observations and comments as He went along, spewing wrath-filled statements? Condemning Judas? Denouncing Pilate?

No, of course not! There is no such record. We are talking about the very conduct of God; and God just would not do that. He was the Lord of Glory. Those things were gone forever after the resurrection. He did not go back and relive those horrible hours, expressing again every emotion and trauma. *Neither should any other man who has thus been crucified.* Never in time, nor in eternity, did Jesus Christ ever refer to the treatment he received at His crucifixion. He lived without a past!

One day you will get a cross. It will come again and again. Each time it will be longer, more trying, more purging. One day you will be dealt a crucifixion: hard, cold, cruel, unjust and possibly public. When it is over, you have a choice. You can drag it along with you the rest of your life, out of your past, into your present, and then into your future.

Of course there is another way.

If you forget the thing, no matter how hideous, the Lord will bring life out of that tomb. You will stand where you have never stood before—higher, holier, stronger. Leave your past where it belongs: in the grave. Whatever black mischief brought on that crucifixion now lies—forgotten—in the grave.

A new breed of men is needed on this earth. Men like the ones we have talked of in these messages. (When we have such *men,* following hard behind them will be the *church* as we have all envisioned her.) These are men who die to themselves, circumstances, logic, injustice, the scriptural right to retaliate; men who walk with near perfect conduct, who have nothing to do with the religious system, but who do not pour hate on it. These are men with utter openness to all Christians, with a pure and undefiled heart; men who know Christ and nothing but Christ, when there is

210

so much that could be known. Men who love the church with a passion, men who can lay down their work; undefending men who never engage in religious controversy, men who get crucified, mouths closed. These are men who never employ "the tools of the trade." Resurrected men!

Out of such a little dying will come so great an amount of life! The world waits for seed that went to death . . . to come alive again. But more: The Lord waits for a people with eyes on the summit. See how high, how very high it is. See how long it has been since feet have trod on some of those ridges.

We may regain the high and lofty heights where those noble men once staked the standard. We may not. But let us agree today: Our intention is to take the banner all the way to the top. Failing that, we just as earnestly desire to carry it far beyond that point where others took it. At the least, we wish to carry it up higher for the next generation to go on beyond us, on to higher, better ground.

If God be pleased, if it be His sovereign design and if grace endures, we offer ourselves—a corporate, living sacrifice—to this end.

Lord!!! May *this* be our mission!

Books you might like to read.

RADICAL BOOKS FOR RADICAL READERS

Beyond Radical

A simple, historical introduction into how we got all of our present-day Christian practices.

You will be thunderstruck to discover that there is really nothing we are doing today in our church practice that came directly out of man's determination to be scriptural. Virtually everything we do came into being sometime during church history, after the New Testament. We have spent the rest of our time trying to bend the Scripture to justify the practice.

When the Church was Led only by Laymen

The word *elder* appears in the New Testament seventeen times, the word *pastor* appears only once (and nobody knows what that word had reference to, because there is no place in the first-century story in which he is clearly seen.)

But there are over one hundred and thirty references from the day of Pentecost forward that refer to either "brothers" or "brothers and the sisters" (Greek: *Adolphus*). *These* were the people who were leading the church. There are only two major players, from a human viewpoint, upon the first-century stage. They are the church planters and God's people - the brothers and sisters. Everything else is a footnote.

BOOKS WHICH SHOW WHAT THE CHRISTIAN FAITH WAS LIKE "FIRST-CENTURY STYLE"

Revolution, the Story of the Early Church
The Silas Diary
The Titus Diary
The Timothy Diary
The Priscilla Diary
The Gaius Diary

The Story! Perhaps the best way we will ever understand what it was like from the day of Pentecost in 30 A.D. until the close of the first century is simply to know the story. Allow yourself to be treated to, and enthralled by that story. (Warning: Knowing the story will change your life forever.) You will find that story in every detail, with nothing missing, in these *six* books.

New Testament
The Story of My Life as told by
Jesus Christ

Matthew, Mark, Luke and John combined into one complete gospel written in first-person singular.

Acts in First-Person

Beginning with Acts 1, Peter tells the story of Acts through chapter 11. Then Barnabas, speaking in first person, tells the story of Acts from chapter 13 to chapter 15. You then hear Silas, Timothy and Luke continue the story all the way through, ending with chapter 28.

Books which show you how to experience Christ

The following books serve as an introduction to the deeper Christian life:

Living by the Highest Life
The Secret to the Christian Life
The Inward Journey

Books that heal

Here are books that have been used all over the world, and in many languages, to heal Christians from the deep, deep pains they experiences as they go through life. Some were written for Christians who have been damaged by their churches and damaged by other Christians. Others are books which help you understand the ways of God as they are know working in your life. All of these books are known and loved around the world.

A Tale of Three Kings

A study in brokenness based on the story of Saul, David and Absalom.

The Prisoner in the Third Cell

A study in the mysteries of God's ways, especially when He works contrary to all your understanding and expectations of Him.

Exquisite Agony

Pain suffered by a Christian at the hands of another believer is one of the most destructive experiences one will ever know, let this book start the healing.

Letters to a Devastated Christian

This book explores different techniques practiced by Christian groups who demand extreme submission and passivity from their members. It faces the difficult task of dealing with bitterness and resentment and rebuilding of faith and trust.

SeedSowers

P.O. Box 3317, Jacksonville, FL 32206
800-228-2665
904-598-3456 (fax)   www.seedsowers.com

REVOLUTIONARY BOOKS ON CHURCH LIFE

How to Meet In Homes *(Edwards)* 10.95
An Open Letter to House Church Leaders *(Edwards)* 4.00
When the Church Was Led Only by Laymen *(Edwards)* 4.00
Beyond Radical *(Edwards)* 5.95
Rethinking Elders *(Edwards)* 9.95
Revolution, The Story of the Early Church *(Edwards)* 8.95
The Silas Diary *(Edwards)* 9.99
The Titus Diary *(Edwards)* 8.99
The Timothy Diary *(Edwards)* 9.99
The Priscilla Diary *(Edwards)* 9.99
The Gaius Diary *(Edwards)* 10.99
Overlooked Christianity *(Edwards)* 14.95
Pagan Christianity *(Viola)* 13.95

AN INTRODUCTION TO THE DEEPER CHRISTIAN LIFE

Living by the Highest Life *(Edwards)* 10.99
The Secret to the Christian Life *(Edwards)* 8.99
The Inward Journey *(Edwards)* 8.99

CLASSICS ON THE DEEPER CHRISTIAN LIFE

Experiencing the Depths of Jesus Christ *(Guyon)* 8.95
Practicing His Presence *(Lawrence/Laubach)* 8.95
The Spiritual Guide *(Molinos)* 8.95
Union With God *(Guyon)* 8.95
The Seeking Heart *(Fenelon)* 9.95
Intimacy with Christ *(Guyon)* 10.95
The Song of the Bride *(Guyon)* 9.95
Spiritual Torrents *(Guyon)* 10.95
The Ultimate Intention *(Fromke)* 10.00

IN A CLASS BY ITSELF

The Divine Romance *(Edwards)* 8.99

NEW TESTAMENT

The Story of My Life as told by Jesus Christ *(Four gospels blended)* 14.95
Acts in First-Person *(Book of Acts)* 9.95

COMMENTARIES BY JEANNE GUYON

Genesis Commentary 10.95
Exodus Commentary 10.95
Leviticus - Numbers - Deuteronomy Commentaries 12.95
Judges Commentary 7.95
Job Commentary 10.95
Song of Songs *(Song of Solomon Commentary)* 9.95
Jeremiah Commentary 7.95
James - I John - Revelation Commentaries 12.95

The Chronicles Heaven *(Edwards)*

The Beginning 8.99
The Escape 8.99
The Birth 8.99
The Triumph 8.99
The Return 8.99

The Collected works of T. Austin-Sparks

The Centrality of Jesus Christ 19.95
The House of God 29.95
Ministry 29.95
Service 19.95
Spiritual Foundations 29.95
The Things of the Spirit 10.95
Prayer 14.95
The On-High Calling 10.95
Rivers of Living Water 8.95
The Power of His Resurrection 8.95

Comfort and healing

A Tale of Three Kings *(Edwards)* 8.99
The Prisoner in the Third Cell *(Edwards)* 5.99
Letters to a Devastated Christian *(Edwards)* 7.95
Exquisite Agony *(Edwards)* 8.95
Dear Lillian *(Edwards)* 5.95

Other books on church life

Climb the Highest Mountain *(Edwards)* 10.99
The Torch of the Testimony *(Kennedy)* 14.95
The Passing of the Torch *(Chen)* 9.95
Going to Church in the First Century *(Banks)* 5.95
When the Church was Young *(Loosley)* 8.95
Church Unity *(Litzman,Nee,Edwards)* 14.95
Let's Return to Christian Unity *(Kurosaki)* 14.95

Christian Living

The Autobiography of Jeanne Guyon 19.95
Final Steps in Christian Maturity *(Guyon)* 12.95
Turkeys and Eagles *(Lord)* 8.95
The Life of Jeanne Guyon *(T.C. Upham)* 17.95
Life's Ultimate Privilege *(Fromke)* 10.00
Unto Full Stature *(Fromke)* 10.00
All and Only *(Kilpatrick)* 7.95
Adoration *(Kilpatrick)* 8.95
Release of the Spirit *(Nee)* 6.00
Bone of His Bone *(Huegel) modernized* 8.95
Rethinking the Wineskin *(Viola)* 8.95
Who is Your Covering? *(Viola)* 6.95

*Prices subject to change